COMPACT

FIRST
FOR SCHOOLS
THIRD EDITION

B2

STUDENT'S BOOK
WITHOUT ANSWERS
WITH DIGITAL PACK

Laura Matthews, Barbara Thomas
and Frances Treloar

Shaftesbury Road, Cambridge CB2 8EA, United Kingdom

One Liberty Plaza, 20th Floor, New York, NY 10006, USA

477 Williamstown Road, Port Melbourne, VIC 3207, Australia

314–321, 3rd Floor, Plot 3, Splendor Forum, Jasola District Centre, New Delhi – 110025, India

103 Penang Road, #05–06/07, Visioncrest Commercial, Singapore 238467

Cambridge University Press & Assessment is a department of the University of Cambridge.

We share the University's mission to contribute to society through the pursuit of education, learning and research at the highest international levels of excellence.

www.cambridge.org
Information on this title: www.cambridge.org/9781009167161

© Cambridge University Press & Assessment 2013, 2014, 2023

This publication is in copyright. Subject to statutory exception and to the provisions of relevant collective licensing agreements, no reproduction of any part may take place without the written permission of Cambridge University Press & Assessment.

First published 2013
Second edition 2014
Third edition 2023

20 19 18 17 16 15 14 13 12 11 10 9 8 7 6 5 4 3 2 1

Printed in Dubai by Oriental Press

A catalogue record for this publication is available from the British Library

ISBN 978-1-009-16716-1 Student's Book without answers with digital pack

Additional resources for this publication at www.cambridge.org/compact

Cambridge University Press & Assessment has no responsibility for the persistence or accuracy of URLs for external or third-party internet websites referred to in this publication and does not guarantee that any content on such websites is, or will remain, accurate or appropriate.

Contents

	Map of the units	4
1	My community	6
2	Home and away	14
3	Performance	22
4	Fit and healthy	30
5	Lessons learnt	38
6	Our planet	46
7	Influences	54
8	Breakthrough	62
	Revision units	70
	Visual materials	78
	Grammar reference	81
	Irregular verbs	95
	Writing bank	96
	Speaking bank	108
	Phrasal verb builder	118
	Wordlist	120
	Exam information	126
	Acknowledgements	127

MAP OF THE UNITS

UNIT	TOPICS	GRAMMAR	VOCABULARY	READING
1 My community	New Year celebrations Friends	Present and future tenses State verbs Comparisons	Words with similar meanings Matching expressions with similar meanings	Part 5: multiple-choice questions
2 Home and away	Adventure and travel Where you live	Adverb formation Past tenses	Word building (1): adjective suffixes (-ed, -ing) Cities, towns and villages	Part 6: gapped text
3 Performance	Music Film and theatre	Linking words The passive	Music Film and cinema	Part 7: multiple matching
4 Fit and healthy	Sport Health	Modal verbs Prepositions: *at*, *in*, *on*	Sport Food Word building (2): noun suffixes (-ence, -ity, -(s/t)ion)	Part 5: multiple-choice questions
5 Lessons learnt	Achievements Education	Conditionals	Phrasal verbs Careers Education	Part 7: multiple matching
6 Our planet	Environment Wildlife	Countable and uncountable nouns Articles *so* and *such* (*a/an*), *too* and *enough*	Climate Environmental problems Animals	Part 6: gapped text
7 Influences	Buying and selling People and feelings	Verbs and expressions followed by *to* + infinitive or -*ing* form Reported speech	Shopping Feelings	Part 5: multiple-choice questions
8 Breakthrough	Technology Science	Relative clauses	Technology Science Word building (3): prefixes and suffixes	Part 7: multiple matching

USE OF ENGLISH	WRITING	LISTENING	SPEAKING
Part 1: multiple-choice cloze	Part 1: Essay understanding the question, paragraphing, linking words and phrases	Part 3: multiple matching	Part 1: leisure activities Part 2: comparing ways of spending free time
Part 2: open cloze Part 3: word formation	Part 2: Story sequencing, using a range of past tenses, adjectives and adverbs	Part 1: multiple-choice questions with short recordings	Part 3: discussing preferences, agreeing and disagreeing Part 4: talking about where you live
Part 4: key-word transformations	Part 2: Review organising paragraphs, recommending, using linking words and phrases	Part 4: multiple-choice questions with long recording	Part 1: adding extra information and comments Part 2: talking about films and music, avoiding unknown words, giving preferences
Part 2: open cloze Part 3: word formation	Part 2: Email and letter giving advice, making suggestions, persuading, beginnings and endings	Part 2: sentence completion	Part 3: asking for and reacting to opinions Part 4: discussing sports and keeping fit
Part 1: multiple-choice cloze Part 4: key-word transformations	Part 2: Article keeping the reader's attention, describing and linking	Part 2: sentence completion	Part 1: discussing ambitions, achievements and education Part 2: making guesses
Part 2: open cloze	Part 2: Review understanding the question, recommending	Part 4: multiple-choice questions with long recording	Part 3: agreeing, disagreeing, making a comment or suggestion Part 4: discussing ways of helping the environment
Part 4: key-word transformations	Part 2: Email and letter giving information, using linking words and phrases	Part 3: multiple matching	Part 1: expressing likes and dislikes Part 2: comparing different ways of shopping
Part 3: word formation	Part 1: Essay using a range of vocabulary	Part 1: multiple-choice questions with short recordings	Part 3: structuring a conversation Part 4: discussing technology

1 My community

NEW YEAR CELEBRATIONS

Listening

1 Look at the photos. They all show people celebrating New Year.

1. Do you think all the photos are of people in the same country? Why? / Why not?
2. How do you think the people in the photos are feeling?

2 In pairs, answer the following questions.

1. Do you celebrate New Year? If so, when and how do you celebrate? If not, what other time of year do you celebrate? How do you celebrate?
2. Why do you think it is important for people to celebrate at the beginning of a new year?

Part 3

3 🔊 02 Listen to Anita talking about what she did to celebrate New Year. Answer these questions.

1. Who did she spend the evening with?
2. What did she learn about?
3. Was everything the same as usual for her on New Year's Eve?

4 🔊 02 Listen again. What does Anita say about her family's celebration? Choose one answer from A–C. Your answers in Exercise 3 will help you.

A I found out about our traditions.
B Everything that evening was just the same as usual for me.
C An activity gave me a better understanding of people I was with.

✓ Exam task

The task below is shorter than in the exam. In Listening Part 3 you hear five speakers and you select the correct answer from a choice of eight possible statements. You have already heard Anita. Now you will hear two more people.

🔊 03 You will hear two people talking about how they celebrated New Year. Choose from the list **A–D** what each speaker says about how they celebrated it.

A I found out about our traditions.
B I was affected by thoughts about a future celebration.
C An activity gave me a better understanding of people I was with.
D I discussed my ambitions for the coming year.

Speaker 1 ....   Speaker 2 ....

💡 Exam tips

- A statement may refer to particular parts of what the speaker says or it may refer to what the speaker says as a whole. You need to listen for both details and for general meaning.
- In the exam, you will hear each recording twice, so don't worry if you don't get all the answers the first time.

Reading and Use of English

Part 1

Vocabulary – Words with similar meanings

1 Work in pairs. Look at the verbs in the box and think about how their meanings are different. Complete the definitions (1–4), then the example sentence (5), with the correct verb. Use one verb twice.

> distinguish   enhance   expose   highlight

1 To .... means to see the difference between two things.
2 To .... means to attract attention to something.
3 To .... means to make something seem better.
4 To .... means to make public something bad or dishonest.
5 My sisters are twins, so it's hard to .... one from the other.

💡 Exam tip

Reading and Use of English Part 1 tests mainly the meaning of vocabulary, but some items will test the grammar of the gapped sentences, too.

2 Sometimes you need to look at the grammar of the sentence as well as the meaning of the word. Choose the correct word for each gap. The important grammar in these sentences is <u>underlined</u>.

> consisted   contributed   involved   participated

1 I had an awful burger that .... <u>of</u> just a thin piece of dry, minced meat in a stale bread bun.
2 Hari won't <u>be</u> .... <u>in</u> organising the end-of-term celebrations as he's on holiday.
3 Nisha .... her pocket money <u>to</u> the collection for the teacher's present.
4 All the students in my class .... <u>in</u> the beach clean-up.

3 Quickly read the text in the exam task. Answer these questions.

1 When does International Youth Day happen?
2 What kind of events happen to celebrate International Youth Day?

✓ Exam task

For questions **1–8**, read the text below and decide which answer (**A**, **B**, **C** or **D**) best fits each gap. There is an example at the beginning (**0**).

International Youth Day

The United Nations (UN) organisation held the first International Youth Day (IYD) in 1991. It is celebrated on 12th August each year, and its aims are both to support young people and (0) .... the benefits they bring to society.

The UN **(1)** .... 'youth' as 15–24 year olds. This age group makes up one-sixth of the human population, and is growing **(2)** .... The UN believes it is **(3)** .... that young people are given the tools to enable them to play a major **(4)** .... in their own development, as well as that of their communities. IYD helps to make this happen.

On the day, young people across the world **(5)** .... in events. There are usually youth conferences on issues connected to the IYD **(6)** ...., which changes each year. In 2021, for instance, it was 'Transforming Food Systems: Youth Innovation for Human and Planetary Health.' **(7)** .... conferences, there are also concerts, sporting events, parades and mobile exhibitions that **(8)** .... young people's achievements.

0	A market	B promote	C drive	D push
1	A outlines	B specifies	C expresses	D defines
2	A rapidly	B completely	C widely	D heavily
3	A significant	B central	C vital	D compulsory
4	A function	B role	C task	D position
5	A attend	B participate	C involve	D contribute
6	A matter	B theory	C case	D theme
7	A Concerning	B Despite	C Besides	D Among
8	A distinguish	B enhance	C highlight	D expose

4 Read the text again and your answers. Check that you have thought about the differences in meaning between each one.

UNIT 1   7

Speaking

Part 1
>> Page 108

1 🔊 04 Look at the Speaking Part 1 questions and the possible answers in the table below. Listen to Luca and Julie answering the questions. Note down the extra information they add.

Question	Answer	Extra information
1 Do you do any activities after school?	play tennis	
2 When do you do your homework?	after dinner	
3 What do you usually do at the weekend?	meet friends, see grandmother	
4 What are you going to do next weekend?	friends, shopping, piano	

2 🔊 04 Complete these sentences from the recording. Listen again if you need to.

1 I .... to play tennis.
2 When I .... home from school, I .... video games.
3 On Saturday I .... to town.
4 We .... shopping.
5 I .... my piano most of the day.
6 I .... in a concert next Thursday.

✓ Exam task

Now work with a partner and ask and answer the questions in Exercise 1.

💡 Exam tip

You will get more marks if you add some detail. To expand your answers, think about why, when and how you do things.

Part 2
>> Page 110

3 Look at photographs A and B. Which of the following adjectives, verbs, nouns and expressions could you use to talk about them?

> a quiet spot bored chat concentrate
> countryside crowded energetic excited
> exercise fresh air in the distance
> in the shade indoors lazy outdoors relax

4 Think of the advantages of spending your time like the people in these two photographs.

🔊 05 Listen to Julie's answer. Does she give the same advantages as you?

✓ Exam task

Work in pairs. Look at photographs A and B above, and 1 and 2 on page 9. Take turns to talk about your photographs and compare them. Time yourselves. Try to talk for about one minute each and answer this question.

> For the people, what are the advantages of spending their free time in these ways?

💡 Exam tip

The question you have to answer is printed above the photographs in the exam. Make sure you answer this question when you are talking.

When you have finished, ask your partner this question. In the exam you have about 30 seconds to answer.

> Which of these things would you prefer to do with your friends? Why?

FRIENDS

Grammar

Present and future tenses
Page 81

1. Work in pairs. Look at the tenses Luca and Julie use to talk about the present and future in Exercise 2 on page 8.
   1. Which tense does Luca use when he talks about playing tennis?
   2. Which tense does he use for the things he does regularly?
   3. Julie uses two different tenses to talk about next Saturday. Why?
   4. Why does she use a continuous tense to talk about playing the piano on Sunday?
   5. Which tense does she use to talk about the concert? Is it definitely happening?

2. Look at the sentences below. Which is correct, A or B?

A	B
I like to relax.	I'm liking to relax.
I prefer to do my homework after dinner.	I'm preferring to do my homework after dinner.
I know I need to practise.	I'm knowing I need to practise.

   What do you notice about the verbs *like*, *prefer* and *know*? Can you think of other verbs which behave in the same way?

3. Choose the correct answer.
   1. I **want** / **'m wanting** to go to France next year.
   2. I **usually stay** / **'m usually staying** with my grandparents during the summer.
   3. Mark, can I choose the café where we **meet** / **'re meeting** tomorrow?
   4. Next Sunday we **go** / **'re going** to an Italian restaurant.
   5. I **'m thinking** / **think** we should go skiing next year.
   6. We will be hungry when we **arrive** / **'ll arrive** at the hotel.
   7. I can't come to your house because I **'ll have** / **'m having** dinner with my family.
   8. I'll make my lunch tomorrow morning before I **'ll leave** / **leave** the house.
   9. I **write** / **'m writing** this text to let you know that I **arrive** / **'m going to arrive** on Saturday.
   10. I'm very excited that we **go** / **'re going** on holiday next month.

Comparisons
Page 82

4. These sentences make comparisons with different adjectives and nouns. Put the words in italics in the correct order to make sentences about photographs A and B on page 8.
   1. The people in the first photograph *much / than / probably / are / happier* the person in the second one.
   2. They *more / than / will / time / spend / walking* doing an online workout.
   3. The person in the second photo is indoors, which *enjoyable / being / as / isn't / as* in the fresh air.
   4. They *getting / exercise / probably / more / are /*.
   5. He *than / energetic / is / more / being* the people in the first photograph.

5. Look at the two photos below. Write two or three sentences comparing them, using some of these words.

   expensive   far more   fun   interesting   much less   thrilling

Reading and Use of English

Vocabulary – Matching expressions with similar meanings

1 To answer multiple-choice questions in the Reading test, you need to find words in the text with a similar meaning to words in the options. Read the first paragraph of the text and find words or phrases which match the expressions below.

1 not confident ....
2 because of ....
3 type of personality ....
4 people in a book or film ....
5 group ....
6 become aware of doing something without intending to ....
7 a worry ....

Part 5

2 Look at the photo and answer these questions with a partner.

1 What do you think the relationship is between these people? Why?
2 What are they doing?
3 What do you think the person taking the photo will do with it? Why will they want to do this?

> **Exam tip**
>
> Before you answer the questions, always read the title and text quickly to get an idea of what it is about.

3 Read the title and text very quickly and answer these questions.

1 Which of these is the main topic of the text?
   A descriptions of the personalities of the writer's friends
   B how the writer and others feel about their friendships
2 Whose words does the writer quote?

> **Exam task**

In Reading and Use of English Part 5, there are always six multiple-choice questions about one text. The text here is shorter than in the exam, and there are only four questions.

For questions **1–4** on page 11, choose the answer (**A**, **B**, **C** or **D**) which you think fits best according to the text.

http://www.friendship.blogspot

Having enough friends

Do you ever find yourself wondering why you don't have as many fabulous friends as other people seem to have? I do. But that's my nature. Whether it's about school, family or what I'm going to wear, I'll always have anxiety about something! Often, it's about friendships: specifically, whether I have enough of them. Perhaps it's a consequence of my obsession with Young Adult (YA) literature and movies, all of whose main characters seem to have an ever-growing circle of close friends, or it's the fact I can't stop comparing myself to people I follow on social media. Whatever the reasons are, I've long felt insecure about the number of friends I have.

I'm not saying I'm completely friendless – I'm lucky to have the most amazing people in my life, and I wouldn't change them for anything. The issue is that I don't have the large group of friends that we're led to believe is what we should all aim for. I have several little groups of friends – one from school, one from my basketball team, one from my early childhood and so on. Having all these relationships in separate areas of my life is great, and yet I sometimes feel they might not be enough.

When I brought the topic of friendships up with some classmates, I was relieved to find that other people feel just like I do. My friend Lyla told me, 'As I've got older, I've found that I've lost friendships. The ones I've kept are stronger than ever, but many of my friends are at different schools, and some are living in other towns. Plus, most of my friends now aren't friends with each other – they don't even know one another, and have only met at my birthday parties, so apart from that, I never arrange to see them all at once. I regret

Reading and Use of English

not having something like my older brother has – he regularly meets up with a huge gang of mates he's had since primary-school days!'

Another of my friends, Jonathan, shares a similar feeling, though he's had a different life experience so far from Lyla and me. 'Because of my mum's job, I've lived in five cities and three countries since I was born, which means I've had loads of practice at making friends,' Jonathan says. 'It's something I've always focused on, investing loads of time and energy into forming friendships through school, neighbours and friends of friends. But this means I have 'pockets' of friends all over the place.' He added, 'I do sometimes envy people who have a big circle of close friends who all know each other and meet up regularly, with a long, shared history and plenty of in-jokes.'

For me, other people's reflections on friendships have been extremely helpful. Friendships play a massive role in our lives, so it's not surprising that we're so concerned about how successful we are at forming and maintaining them.

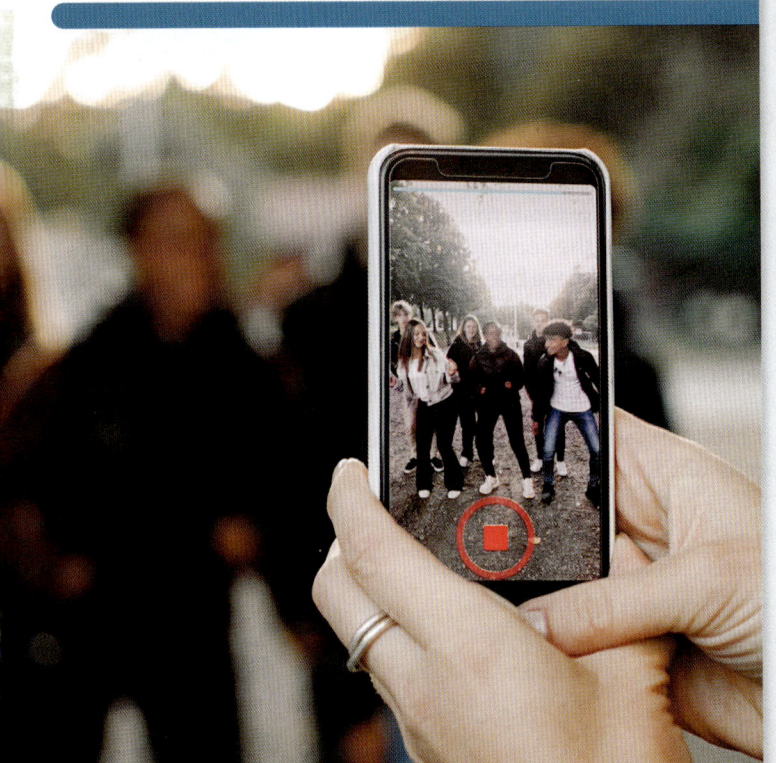

1 Before you answer this question, underline where in the text YA literature is mentioned. Carefully read the text before it as well as after it. The vocabulary exercise on page 10 will help you.

In the first paragraph, the writer says that Young Adult literature has been
- A one of the inspirations for her approach to making new friends.
- B a source of comfort to her when experiencing friendship difficulties.
- C one possible cause of her tendency to worry about friendships.
- D an influence that led her to develop more friendships online.

2 Some questions ask you about the function of a paragraph – what the writer does in it. Pay close attention to the first word of each option in this question and read the whole paragraph before deciding which the writer is doing.

What is the writer doing in the second paragraph?
- A listing the areas of her life where she lacks friendships
- B outlining a disadvantage of having lots of friends
- C explaining the exact nature of her dissatisfaction
- D describing how other people regard her friendship

3 Some questions focus on what people quoted in the text think about something. Find the quote from Lyla and underline words and phrases which show what she thinks.

What does Lyla say about friendships?
- A Losing some friends is a normal part of growing up.
- B The friendships you form when you are children are the strongest.
- C It is highly unlikely that all your friends will get on well with each other.
- D Her brother's friendship group is an example of what she would like.

4 Some questions ask you about what you learn from a section of text. Find what Jonathan says and underline key words and phrases in the options and in the text. Then try to match meanings – the best match between option and text will be the answer!

What do we learn about Jonathan from what he says?
- A He is glad to be able to see his friends so often.
- B He feels lucky to have friends in so many different places.
- C He has found it difficult to keep in touch with all his friends.
- D He sees having friends as an important part of his life.

UNIT 1 11

Writing

Part 1 essay
>> Page 96

1. Work in pairs. Describe your family. Which members of your family are most important to you? Why?

2. Talk about your friends. Do you have lots of friends, or just a few good ones? Where did you meet them?

3. Answer these questions. Write A for family, B for friends or C for both.

Who:	takes care of you?	☐
	gives you advice?	☐
	teaches you to do things?	☐
Who do you:	have most fun with?	☐
	spend most time with?	☐
	get on best with?	☐

✓ Exam task

4. Now read the exam task and answer the true/false questions below with your partner.

   True or false?
   1. You have a choice of question in Part 1 of the Writing paper.
   2. You must write an essay of at least 190 words.
   3. The first sentence of the task helps you to understand what you must write about.
   4. You are asked to compare two things in this essay.
   5. You should write about young people in general, and not just yourself.
   6. When you give 'your own idea' it should be different from points 1 and 2 in the notes.

You **must** answer this question. Write your answer in **140–190** words in an appropriate style on the separate answer sheet.
In your English class you have been talking about your family and friends. Now your English teacher has asked you to write an essay for homework.
Write your essay using **all** the notes and giving reasons for your point of view.

Which is more important to young people: their family or their friends?
Notes
Write about:
1 who teenagers spend most time with
2 who gives teenagers most support
3 (your own idea)

Writing

5 Read the model answer to the exam question and then complete the table and answer the questions below with your partner.

By the time they are about 14, young people probably spend more time with their friends than with their family. They are at school every day and therefore in the company of their friends. In addition, they play sport with these friends, go into town with them or go round to their houses at the weekend.

Yet all young people still rely heavily on their families, and their parents especially, for support and advice. Parents have more experience and more knowledge to share than friends, and can help with important decisions. For many people family are always part of their life. In contrast, some friendships can get forgotten as people get older.

In general though, I would say that most young people get on better with their friends than their families. They are the same age; for that reason they often share the same tastes in music and clothes and so on. As for ideas, those are often similar too. As a result, parents are often much less important to their children at this stage.

Overall, I personally think that for most teenagers, their friends are more important than their family.

Which is more important to teenagers: family or friends?	
Main points	
1 who teenagers spend most time with	friends
2 who gives teenagers most support	
3 own idea	
Conclusion	

Is the essay written in a formal or informal style?

6 Find these linking expressions in the model answer and underline them.

> as a result   as for   for that reason   in addition
> in contrast   in general   overall   therefore   yet

7 Now choose the correct linking expressions below.

I love going out with my friends but **(1) in addition / in general** the rest of my family aren't as sociable as me. **(2) As for / Yet** my grandparents, they're much happier at home. **(3) In other words / In fact**, they're always busy as they've got lots of hobbies. **(4) For that reason / For example**, I always ring them before I go there in case they're in the middle of doing something. **(5) Yet / Therefore** if I do just turn up, they don't mind. **(6) Nevertheless / In contrast**, my friend's grandparents are always going away so she hardly ever sees them.

8 Read the exam task and plan your answer. When you have finished, discuss your ideas with a partner. Then do the task.

💡 Exam tips

- It is important to decide what you are going to say in your essay before you start writing. In the exam, you can write your plan on the exam paper.
- When you have finished writing, read your essay carefully to check for grammar and spelling mistakes.

✓ Exam task

Answer this question. Write your answer in **140–190** words in an appropriate style.
In your English class you have been talking about where to live after leaving your family home. Now your English teacher has asked you to write an essay for homework. Write your essay using **all** the notes and giving reasons for your point of view.
When a young person goes to university, should they live at home or in student accommodation with friends?
Notes
Write about:
1 support
2 being independent
3 (your own idea)

UNIT 1   13

2 Home and away

ADVENTURE AND TRAVEL

Reading and Use of English

1. **Look at the young people in the photos. Work in pairs to answer the questions.**
   1. Which picture shows: base jumping, polar trekking, rock climbing?
   2. Would you like to do any of these activities? Why? / Why not?
   3. How do you think they prepared before doing these things?

Part 6

2. **Look at the text opposite. Read it quickly to answer the following question.**

   What do teenage students do if they are selected for the Nordic Exploration Club?

   > 💡 **Exam tip**
   >
   > When you are matching a missing sentence with a section of text, look for different words and phrases that refer to the same thing or person.

3. **Read the text again. Write what or who the bolded phrases refer to.**
   1. the explorer ....
   2. the organisation ....
   3. participants ....
   4. the expedition itself ....
   5. the whole experience ....
   6. the young people ....

4. **Find the pronouns underlined in the text. Write what they refer to.**
   1. this = ...
   2. it = ...
   3. where = ...
   4. others = ...
   5. their = ...

The Nordic Exploration Club

On visits to schools to give talks about exploring the North Atlantic, Gemma Mann observed that many teenagers had very little self-confidence and lacked motivation. **The explorer** decided to do something to address <u>this</u>, and so the Nordic Exploration Club was born.

The organisation visits schools and selects 14–16-year-old students on the basis of who could benefit most from journeying across the North Atlantic – Iceland and Greenland. Once selected for <u>it</u>, **participants** undergo a tough and lengthy training programme. **The expedition itself** involves a trip to Iceland, and then on to Greenland, <u>where</u> they spend ten days navigating through some of the world's remotest Arctic terrain.

The whole experience positively changes the lives of **the young people** as well as <u>others</u> around them. On their return home, they share their stories of the trek with thousands of school children in <u>their</u> region. They are living, breathing proof that dreams are attainable and that ordinary teenagers can achieve something truly extraordinary.

Reading and Use of English

Exam task

You are going to read a text about a child who climbed a very high cliff of rock. Six sentences have been removed from the text. Choose from the sentences **A–G** the one which fits each gap (**1–6**). There is one extra sentence which you do not need to use.

Climbing El Capitan at ten years old

Ascending any of the routes on El Capitan, a cliff of rock rising nearly 1,000 metres above Yosemite National Park in the USA, is a demanding task for even the most experienced of climbers. Selah Schneiter from Colorado, however, managed the feat when she was just ten years old.

Selah was no stranger to El Capitan: the site, her father Mike said, was 'in her blood'. He's a climbing guide and instructor, and he'd initially taken his daughter there when she was two months old. **1** ☐ In the process, they'd fallen in love so it seems Selah was connected to the Yosemite rock even before she was born.

Selah's achievement on El Capitan led to a flurry of media attention and TV appearances in New York. Coming from a small town in Colorado, city life in the spotlight was sometimes a struggle for her. **2** ☐ In fact, the thing that she was most concerned about was the possibility of not reaching her goal. Ultimately, her determination proved stronger than any fear. At particularly dangerous points, she took a deep breath and thought: 'What does this mean to me? Am I gonna bail or am I not gonna bail?' Clearly, she didn't 'bail', and on making it to the top, she cried happy tears.

Selah and Mike climbed with a friend, Mark Regier, and the three of them didn't rush to the top, according to Mike. **3** ☐ By Mike's standards, this was a fairly relaxed schedule.

Selah made her way up the 1,000-metre route – a particularly challenging one known as the Nose – primarily by jumaring, which essentially means pulling yourself up a rope. Only a handful of people have ever made 'free climbing' ascents of the Nose, when the climber uses hands and feet on the rock while attached to a rope purely as protection against falls. **4** ☐ It's a piece of kit used by climbers on routes that take several days. This may sound pretty terrifying to non-climbers, but as a climbing guide, Mike is used to the risks of the sport, and they didn't seem to trouble Selah. 'Oddly, we never felt really in danger at any point. We felt really comfortable up there,' Mike said.

When they finally reached the top, they received a surprising text from Joy, Selah's mum. A friend who wrote for *Outside* magazine had investigated the matter and identified Selah as the youngest ever to have scaled El Capitan. **5** ☐ 'Don't even look it up,' he told her. 'We don't want that to be our motivation.'

After the climb, though, Mike realised how inspiring his daughter's story could be to young people, which is why he and Selah gave interviews to news organisations around the world. **6** ☐ 'If you have a big goal, it's really hard to attack it all at once. You have to do it piece by piece. Take that big goal and make it into a bunch of small goals.' She adds that when you're climbing, it helps if 'you look up a lot more than you look down'.

A They spent five days on the climb, taking long lunch breaks and starting as late as seven.

B In one, Selah had wise words for anyone facing a challenging or frightening task.

C She was less bothered by the climb itself, however.

D She says it's hard to remember a time when she didn't love grabbing a rope and heading up a rock.

E At night, father and daughter slept on a portaledge, a tent-like device that hangs off the rock.

F It was also the first place Mike and Selah's mother, Joy, had climbed together.

G Before the climb, Mike had warned Selah against focusing on setting a record.

5 Work in pairs. Which words in the text and sentences helped you decide your answers? Which sentence didn't you use and why?

UNIT 2 | 15

Speaking

WHERE YOU LIVE

Part 3
💬 >> Page 114

1 Think about a city or town you know or have visited. Tick (✓) the places you go/went to.

> café   cinema   museum
> shopping mall   swimming pool   theatre

Write them in order of importance for you (most important = 1). Add any other leisure facilities you use regularly. Which do you think are most popular with young people? Why?

2 Compare your lists in a group. Use some of these expressions.

> I think … is the most/least important because …
> For me, … is less important than … because …
> I'd prefer to go to / I'd rather go to … than … because …
> I would like to … but we don't have one.

3 Are there enough things for young people to do in your area? Which things would you like to be able to do?

4 Think about how you will agree and disagree with the others. Mark these expressions A (agree) or D (disagree).

> I agree with you.
> I think it would be better to …
> That's what I think too.
> I think you're right.
> I disagree.

✓ Exam task

Work in groups of three. The local council in your town wants to build new leisure facilities for young people. Here are some of the places that the council might build. Talk to each other about whether the places would be popular with teenagers.

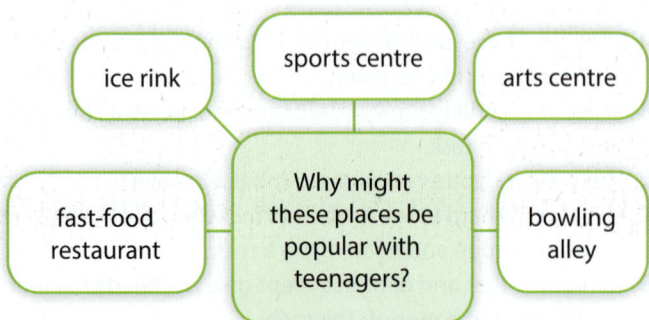

Now decide which two places should be built.

Part 4
💬 >> Page 116

5 Do you live in a city, town or village? Tick (✓) the words and expressions below you can use to talk about it.

> a lot of traffic   by a lake   capital   crowded   farming
> historic   in an area called …   in the centre of …
> in the countryside   in the middle of nowhere
> in the mountains   industrial   isolated
> medium-sized   mining   modern   mountain
> not far from …   on the coast   quiet
> rural   sleepy   university   wide streets

6 Use the words and expressions from Exercise 5 to answer these questions.

1 How would you describe your city/town/village?

> I live in an industrial city.
>
> My village is quite isolated.

2 What do you like about the place where you live? What do you dislike about it?

> I love living on the coast.

✓ Exam task

Practise asking your partner his/her opinion on these questions.

- What's the best thing about living in the middle of a city? Why?
- Do you think it's better to live in a city, or in a village in the countryside? Why?
- Is it better for children to grow up in one place or move around? Why?

💡 Exam tip

It is OK to disagree with each other. The discussion is more important than whether you agree.

Listening

Part 1

1 Work in pairs. Look at the photos below of activities in cities and answer the questions.

1 Are these the kinds of activities tourists usually do when visiting a city? Explain your answer.
2 Which activity do you think looks most exciting? Why?
3 Why do you think these sorts of activities are becoming more common in cities?

2 🔊 06 Listen to a teenager talking about doing a similar activity to one of the photos below. Which activity is he talking about?

Write down all the words which helped you get the answer and compare with your partner.

3 🔊 06 Read the question about the recording. First, try to answer it. Then listen to the recording again and check your answer.

You hear a boy talking about going on a tour in a city.

He says that the only negative aspect of the tour was that the guide

A failed to give enough help to those who were scared of heights.
B tried too hard to make money from participants.
C did too much talking to the group.

4 🔊 06 Listen again and read the script your teacher gives you. Underline the words which give you the answer. Why are the other answers wrong?

✓ Exam task

In Listening Part 1 you hear eight recordings and you answer one question about each. There are only four recordings in the task below.

🔊 07 You will hear people talking in four different situations. For questions **1–4**, choose the best answer (**A**, **B** or **C**).

1 You hear a woman on the radio talking about a basketball exhibition centre. She says it offers visitors the opportunity to
   A meet a player.
   B interact with a coach.
   C practise basketball.

2 You hear two friends talking about Disneyland. What does the boy suggest to the girl?
   A He has never been interested in going to Disneyland.
   B The event she creates may be as good as a trip to Disneyland.
   C He could help make her dream about Disneyland come true.

3 You hear two friends talking about wild camping. What is the boy's attitude towards wild camping?
   A He would only try it under certain conditions.
   B He might prefer it to normal camping.
   C He can see its appeal to some people.

4 You hear a boy talking about travelling. What point is he making?
   A Many people value the idea of adventure too highly.
   B People must switch to greener forms of transport.
   C Young people should consider the impact of trips abroad more.

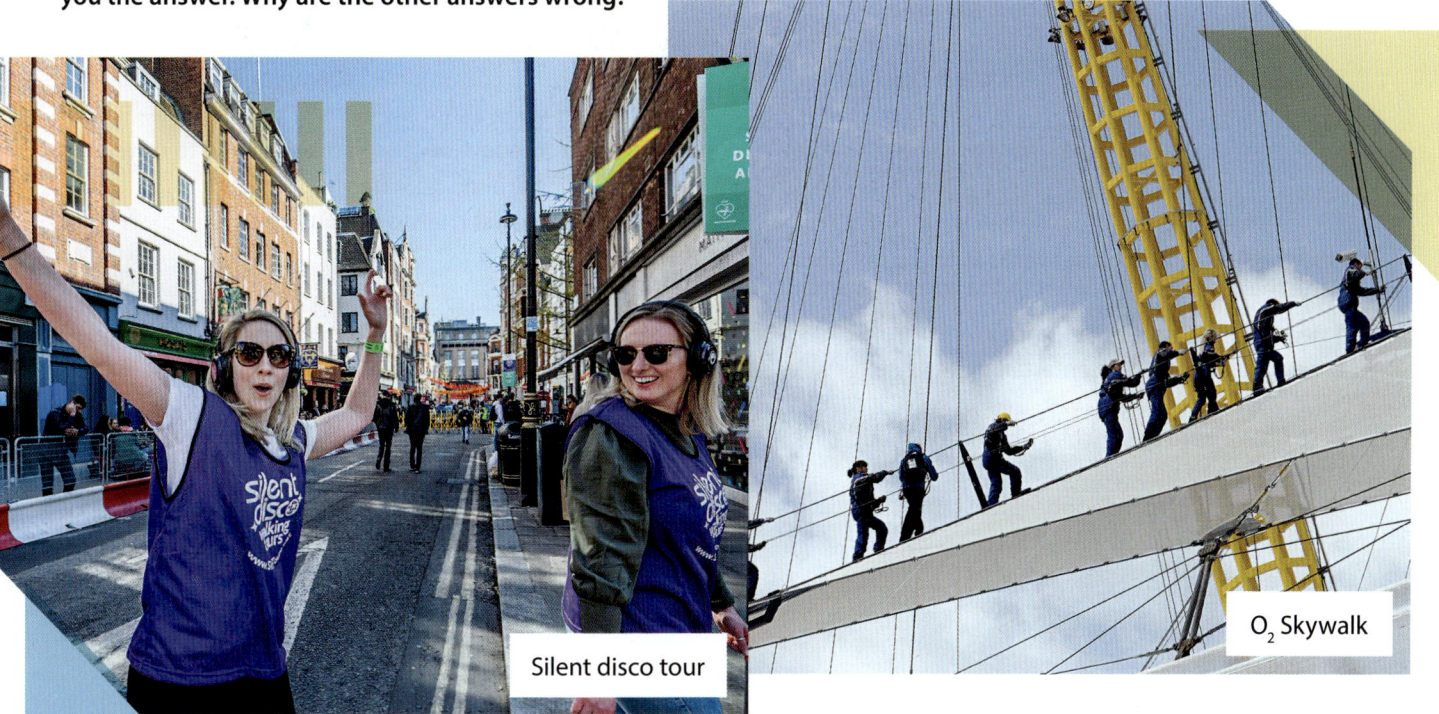

Silent disco tour

O_2 Skywalk

UNIT 2

Reading and Use of English

Part 2

1. Read the text below quickly to find out what it is about. Complete the gaps with prepositions from the box.

   from   of   on   out x2   up x2   with

A city boy who lives in a village

I live in a sleepy little village just outside the city of Bath. When I was growing (1) ...., there was nothing to do except hang (2) .... with friends in the village. Now I spend the majority (3) .... my time in Bath, either working, going to college or socialising. I have a part-time job in a burger restaurant, and I'm studying music technology. I don't play an instrument, I DJ. Obviously, the dream is to be famous, but that's not exactly realistic! I'll probably end (4) .... working in a studio, which is fine. In my free time, I go to mates' houses or go (5) .... to a club in town. The clubs in Bath are not very good but there are quite a few to choose (6) .... Once a month at college, I put (7) .... a music night (8) .... some other DJs.

2. Find the two-word phrasal verbs in Exercise 1 and write them on the lines next to the correct meaning.

   1. leave the house ....
   2. arrange and perform entertainment ....
   3. to finally be in a particular situation without intending to be ....
   4. going through childhood ....
   5. spend time somewhere ....

Exam task

For questions **1–8**, read the text below and think of the word which best fits each gap. Use only one word in each gap. There is an example at the beginning (**0**).

Exam tip

In Reading and Use of English Part 2 you must only write one word in the gap. Do not put a contraction like *didn't* as this is really two words (*did not*).

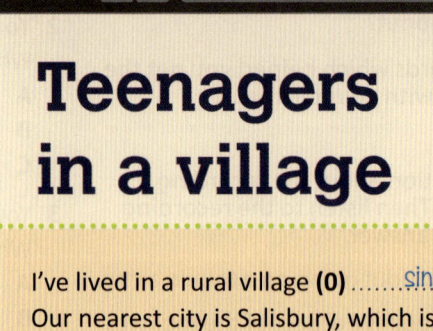

Teenagers in a village

I've lived in a rural village (0) ....*since*.... I was born. Our nearest city is Salisbury, which is (1) .... I now attend school. I've enjoyed growing up here (2) .... the whole. I went to the tiny primary school in my village, which really suited me. So after that, moving to 'big school' in Salisbury, my secondary school, was scary. It was such (3) .... shock to be in classes with so (4) .... unfamiliar people! The best thing (5) .... being a teenager in this kind of location is that life's pretty uncomplicated: you go to school and you hang out with your mates. That's it really! Also, most village residents are friendly and we all look out for each (6) ...., so everyone feels safe. The most difficult thing about my life is (7) .... having much freedom because I'm too young to drive and the bus service around here has (8) .... so unreliable lately that I've stopped using it.

Reading and Use of English

Part 3

Vocabulary – Word building (1)

3 Using the endings in the table, make adjectives from these words. Write them under the best heading. There is one example.

astonish	attach	bother	convince	demand
entertain	exhaust	exist	fascinate
fix	inexperience	irritate	~~terrify~~

-ed	-ing	-ed or -ing
		terrified, terrifying

4 Complete these sentences with an adjective from the table above.

1 The ten km run was so .... in the heat that few of the young runners finished.
2 Maisie and Hulya were .... when they passed the test because they hadn't revised at all.
3 Although Nicola felt completely ...., she jumped into the deep, icy water.
4 Ravi argued a case for meat-eating really well – we all found him very ....
5 The people on the reality show were so silly and .... that I turned it off.

5 When you are deciding between *-ing* or *-ed*, what general rule do you follow?

....

💡 Exam tips

- Each gap has its own word at the end of the line that you must change. Don't try to put that word in any other gap.
- Check your spelling carefully, especially when adding letters to a word ending in *e*!

✓ Exam task

For **1–8**, read the text below. Use the word given in capitals at the end of some of the lines to form a word that fits in the gap in the same line. There is an example at the beginning (**0**).

Going back to my roots

Although I was born in (0) ..*central*.. China, I have no memory of living there because I've lived in New Zealand since my early (1) .... My mum's from Guilin, a city surrounded by (2) .... that's totally unique: steep, rocky hills with pointed peaks and the River Li winding through them. Mum had a painting of this area which I found completely (3) .... when I was younger, and I longed to go there. Last summer, aged 13, my dream became a (4) .... We went on a two-month tour of China, a trip of a (5) .... which included two weeks with an aunt in Guilin. The landscape looked just like the painting! It was (6) .... And so was the food. My aunt's a (7) .... cook, so every dinner was a treat. Afterwards, she'd say, '100 steps after eating is good for the (8) ....,' and we'd walk the streets with the hills lit up in the background. It was magical.

CENTRE

CHILD

SCENE

FASCINATE

REAL

LIFE

BELIEVABLE
TALENT

DIGEST

UNIT 2 19

Grammar

Adverb formation
>> Page 82

1 Make adjectives from these adverbs.

1. bitterly
2. clumsily
3. happily
4. hopefully
5. miserably
6. positively
7. politely
8. rapidly
9. rarely
10. simply

2 Now use the adverbs and adjectives above to answer these questions.

1. Which adjectives change their last letter to -i before adding -ly?
2. What happens to adjectives ending in a consonant and -le?
3. What happens to other adjectives ending in -e?
4. What happens to adjectives ending in -l?

3 Match the correct adjective with the noun in these sentences.

concerning   courageous
interesting   strong

1. It's a(n) .... idea, and I want to see if it works.
2. Lola made a(n) .... attempt to win the competition, but she was beaten in the final.
3. Peter suddenly had a(n) .... thought – what if the homework was due in last week?
4. When I walked into the room, I had a(n) .... sense that something was wrong.

aggressive   detailed
excellent   successful

5. One of the teachers drew up a(n) .... plan which outlined all aspects of history teaching for the year.
6. Max's .... attitude got him into trouble throughout his school years.
7. It was a(n) .... solution to the problem, so we decided to test it straight away.
8. Victoria made a(n) .... attempt on the school shot put record.

4 Choose the correct adverb to go with the verb in these sentences.

1. The head teacher spoke **angrily** / **calmly** to the young girl and she soon settled down.
2. The crowd reacted **positively** / **optimistically** to the team's performance.
3. The man ate **loudly** / **boldly**, which annoyed some people in the restaurant.
4. Patrick ran **awkwardly** / **quickly** and scored the goal that won the match.
5. The parents were pleased that the talent show was run very **efficiently** / **poorly**.
6. My best friend **kindly** / **funnily** offered to pay for my ticket to the cinema.
7. The teacher encouraged his pupils to watch **happily** / **closely** as he completed the experiment.
8. The couple waited **patiently** / **slowly** for their dinner to be brought out.

Past tenses
>> Page 82

a  b  c

5 Read this text about Parker Liautaud and put the verb in brackets into the correct tense (past simple or past perfect).

Parker Liautaud (1) .... (attempt) to reach the North Pole. Two other teenagers (2) .... (reach) the North Pole previously. They (3) .... (travel) with their parents, but Parker (4) .... (go) with a guide called Doug, who (5) .... (be) to the North Pole seven times before. Unfortunately, the cracks in the ice (6) .... (be) too large for them to cross. Doug (7) .... (not see) problems like that before on his other trips. In the end, they (8) .... (fly) the last part of the journey in a helicopter.

6 Choose the correct word or words in these sentences.

1. Last week I went to the cinema and I **'ve watched** / **watched** a funny film.
2. When we **got** / **were getting** home, my father realised he **'d forgotten** / **forgot** to buy some bread.
3. I **finished** / **was finishing** my homework last night.
4. There's nothing to do here during the winter, so we **travelled** / **were travelling** to the city.
5. Yesterday, as I **was coming** / **came** home, I **was finding** / **found** an injured animal.
6. The games console **was sold** / **selling** out before I got to the shop, because everyone else had arrived at opening time.
7. I **'ve been trying** / **tried** to make some lunch since I got home and I still **haven't done** / **didn't do** it.
8. My purse disappeared so I **looked** / **was looking** everywhere for it.

Writing

Part 2 story
>> Page 106

1 You are going to read a story set in a jungle. Read the exam task and the words and phrases below. Tell your partner what you think is going to happen.

> Your English teacher has asked you to write a story for a competition.
> Your story must begin with these words:
> **It was dark and I could hear strange sounds all around me.**
> Your story must include:
> - a jungle
> - treasure
>
> Write your **story**.

> archaeologist   expedition
> fall into a hole   gold   Inca city

2 Stories are usually written in the past tense. Choose the correct form of the past tense verbs in the story.

> It was dark and I could hear strange sounds all around me. I was in the jungle, **(1) looking / looked** for a lost city. Everyone **(2) knew / was knowing** it was there, but no one **(3) had / has** ever found it. The local people told stories of a city full of gold which the Incas **(4) built / had built** centuries ago. Suddenly I **(5) heard / was hearing** a different sound and I **(6) was realising / realised** that it must be Kate. Kate **(7) was / had been** another archaeologist who was part of our expedition. 'Kate, is that you?' I **(8) was calling / called**. 'Yeah, come over here, I **(9) 've / 'd** found a plate or something,' she replied. I **(10) was rushing / rushed** over to find Kate, without looking where I **(11) went / was going** and without warning I **(12) 've disappeared / disappeared** down into a deep hole. Fortunately, I **(13) didn't / haven't** hurt myself. I **(14) got out / had got out** my torch and **(15) shone / was shining** it around the hole. Gold! Piles and piles of gold plates, vases, jewellery, swords! I **(16) 've / 'd** found it – the treasure everyone **(17) had / has** been looking for!

3 Divide the story in Exercise 2 into three paragraphs, one for each section of the story.

4 Here is another exam story question. How will the story continue? How could it end? Discuss your ideas with your partner. Then do the exam task.

Remember to:
- decide on your storyline before you start writing.
- make sure your story follows from the prompt sentence.
- use past tenses and write in paragraphs.
- try to use a range of interesting adjectives, adverbs and collocations.
- write 140–190 words.

✓ Exam task

> Your English teacher has asked you to write a story for a competition.
> Your story must begin with these words:
> **When I was walking home from school, I looked up from my phone and realised I didn't recognise the street I was in!**
> Your story must include:
> - a relative
> - a building
>
> Write your **story** in **140–190** words in an appropriate style.

💡 Exam tip

Your story will read better and get a better mark if you can use some interesting and varied vocabulary and use words that go together well. These are known as collocations.

UNIT 2

3 Performance

MUSIC

Reading and Use of English

1 Underline *two* things in each row that you can see in the photos on pages 22 and 23, then compare your answers with a partner.

1 orchestra	rap artist	punk rock band	jazz band
2 drum kit	keyboard	bass guitar	cello
3 conductor	guitarist	lead singer	backing group
4 microphone	lighting	cables	speakers

2 Which four words or phrases from Exercise 1 are:
1 stage equipment?
2 musical instruments?
3 groups of musicians?
4 individual musicians?

Part 7

3 Read the article about being a professional musician quickly. Match each paragraph with the topic that it is about.

- The advantages of being a musician ☐
- A summary of what the text is about ☐
- The disadvantages of being a musician ☐

4 Match these meanings with words and phrases bolded in the text.
1 makes a piece of music available to the public ....
2 the main rhythm of a piece of music ....
3 a very strong liking ....
4 the words of a song ....
5 newspapers, magazines, TV, radio ....
6 people who write reviews ....

The truth about being a **Professional musician**

BASS GUITARIST **FRANZ MACK** OF **PUNK** BAND LICE tells it like it is

A **(1)** Images of life as a professional musician in **the media** make it seem all about adoring fans, bright lights, and unbelievable luxury. **(2)** Even though I never kidded myself that this was the whole story, when I began my career as a professional bass guitarist, I had a lot to learn about the ups and downs of the path I'd chosen.

B **(3)** There's no short cut to being a skilled guitarist, in spite of any natural talent you may have. **(4)** It takes years of constant effort to get really good, and other areas of your life may suffer. **(5)** While having **a passion** for music will help, it's not enough on its own. **(6)** And when you've made it, you soon find out you can't please everyone. **(7)** The band **releases a track** and, although you think it's your best work, **the critics** say **the beat**'s too slow, or your fans prefer earlier stuff.

C **(8)** However, the deep feeling of connection you experience when playing live to an appreciative audience is mind-blowing. **(9)** Having people yelling along with **the lyrics** while you do what you love best not only feels totally amazing, but it also pushes you to perform beyond what you thought possible. **(10)** It's like nothing else on Earth.

5 Read the text again. Write the number of the sentence or sentences that mention the following:

a a bond between the band and their fans
b something making a performance better than could be imagined
c an incomplete picture of the profession
d people at a concert singing with the band
e some issues that the band's audience might have with the music
f how hard musicians have to work to improve

Reading and Use of English

Careers in music

The music manager

6 Quickly read through the text on the right and decide which section is mainly about the following:

1 becoming a manager through training
2 the income of managers
3 becoming a manager by being one
4 the work responsibilities of most managers
5 a basic explanation of what a music manager is

Exam task

In Reading and Use of English Part 7 there are between four and six texts and you answer ten questions. The texts here are shorter, with only seven questions.

You are going to read an article about being a music manager. For questions **1–7**, choose from the sections **(A–E)**. The sections may be chosen more than once.

In which section does the writer mention

1 the extreme variation in the rewards that different managers may get? ....
2 the manager protecting artists from practical concerns? ....
3 some examples of exceptional managers? ....
4 tasks that the manager does not have to be involved in? ....
5 the need for potential music managers to build a network of contacts? ....
6 how important it is for the manager to be aware of what the intended audience wants? ....
7 the need for managers to take an unemotional approach to their work? ....

A
Behind every top artist or band in the music industry is a hard-working manager. Music management is an incredibly hard and fast-paced career to follow, although it can be very rewarding for those that succeed in it. It is a job that requires experience, creativity, and the ability to negotiate. The usual set up has the manager taking care of business behind the scenes. However, there are a few who have made a name for themselves and are known for their high-profile clientele such as Scooter Braun for Justin Bieber and Ariana Grande, or Troy Carter for Lady Gaga. They are all respected for their organisational skills and how well they understand people in the music industry.

B
The role of a music manager is to organise every aspect of an artist or band's music career, with the exception of writing lyrics and tunes for songs, and the actual recording of the music. That means dealing with live venue appearances, working with record labels, paperwork, logistics, fan-following, booking musical collaborators who match the goals of the artist and the record company, promotions, publicity, and a range of other mundane tasks. By taking care of these things, managers essentially act as a cushion between artists and the demands of the music industry, so that the artists can focus on the art of music-making without any distractions.

C
The sky's the limit when it comes to potential earnings of music managers. However, they have to keep a cool head when it comes to choosing which artists to manage so they can accurately assess how realistic the prospect of success is. If a manager works for a band that has no future, then that manager will be working for almost nothing. This is because most music managers work on commissions rather than a fixed salary amount. In other words, they get paid a certain percentage of however much the artist or band makes. This figure can vary greatly but the standard commission rate ranges from 10 to 20 percent of gross artist revenue.

D
So how does someone become a music manager? No particular qualifications are needed, although a passion for music is essential, and business knowledge and experience of the music industry are beneficial. There are two main pathways to the career. One is through working as an intern or apprentice with existing industry professionals. However, these aren't the kind of posts that will be found in a newspaper or on a job website. To get a post like this, it's vital to work hard at expanding your social circle within the music business so you are at the right place at the right time when something comes up.

E
The other way to become a music manager is to offer your services to an unsigned band or artist. For this, you need to have the skill of recognising true talent. Understanding the music industry and the changes that come within it is fundamental to the manager's role. Knowing what target consumers are looking for in a band or artist, and knowing how to work with your client to give them this is the key to a manager's success.

Listening

FILM AND THEATRE

1 In pairs, look at the photos and say what they show. Then discuss the differences and similarities between the two forms of entertainment and fill in the table. Use words from the box to help your discussion.

> act   audience   camera operator
> costume designer   director   live performance
> on set   on stage   painter   playwright   producer
> recorded on film   scenery   scenes
> scriptwriter   set designer
> sound and lighting technicians   stage manager

	A play	A film
1 who the writer(s) is/are		
2 who's in the cast, what they do, who instructs them		
3 who controls production		
4 who's in the crew, what they do		
5 how, where and by whom it is viewed		

2 Work in pairs. Find the noun from the box which has the same meaning as nouns 1–8.

> an agent   an amateur   a budget   a cast
> innovation   a masterpiece   a production   a viewer

1 creativity ....
2 a show ....
3 a screen-audience member ....
4 a classic ....
5 finances ....
6 a representative ....
7 performers ....
8 a non-professional ....

Part 4

3 Look at the exam task below and the underlining in question 1. Underline two or three important words in the instructions and in the other questions and options.

4 What do you learn from the instructions and the questions about what you will hear? Tick (✓) the topics you expect Rowan to talk about.

a the impact Oakwood School had on him
b which famous people inspired him
c how his skills were developed by Oakwood School
d why he wants to study drama
e the purpose of putting on a certain production
f what he believes is important
g the importance of technicians in productions
h which teacher gave him the most support

✓ Exam task

In Listening Part 4 there are seven multiple-choice questions. In the task below there are four.

🔊 08 You will hear part of a radio interview with a student called Rowan Tate who is talking about how his school helped him get into drama college. For questions 1–4, choose the best answer (**A**, **B** or **C**).

1 How does Rowan say <u>Oakwood School made an impact on him?</u>
   A It gave him <u>his first opportunity to act.</u>
   B It greatly <u>increased</u> his <u>self-confidence.</u>
   C It brought about a <u>change in his attitude.</u>

2 Rowan says that the end-of-year show at the school is intended to
   A appeal equally to professionals and amateurs in the audience.
   B give participants a production experience that is close to professional.
   C achieve a professional standard within a tight budget.

3 What view of the technical side of productions was taught at the school?
   A It is a good choice for further education.
   B It is as important as the acting.
   C It is more demanding than it seems.

4 What did Rowan appreciate about the school trips?
   A the range of artistic work they exposed him to
   B the focus they had on traditional theatre
   C the opportunity they gave him to see live performances

💡 Exam tip

Underlining important words helps you to listen for the answer and predict what you will hear.

Speaking

Part 1
>> Page 108

1 Look at question 1 below and the candidate's answer. Then write your answers for questions 1–6, add extra information and an additional comment and/or opinion.

Films and cinema
1 How often do you watch films?
2 Who do you like watching films with? Why?
3 What is your favourite type of film and why?

Music
4 Have you ever been to a concert? Did you enjoy it?
5 When and how do you like listening to music?
6 Do you play a musical instrument? Which one?

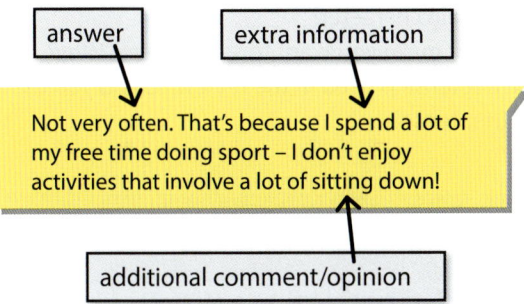

answer → Not very often. ← extra information
That's because I spend a lot of my free time doing sport – I don't enjoy activities that involve a lot of sitting down!
↑ additional comment/opinion

2 Now take it in turns to ask each other the questions.

💡 Exam tip
Don't just give one-word answers. Try to give extra information. Then add a comment or opinion.

Part 2
>> Page 110

3 Work in pairs. Make a list of things you can say about the photos opposite.

4 🔊 09 Now listen to two candidates talking about the photos. Did they have the same ideas as you? Tick (✓) the ideas that are on your list.

5 🔊 09 Listen again. Both the candidates needed words they didn't know. Complete the phrases they used to explain what they meant.

1 … she's wearing you know, some listening ………………
2 … I wouldn't choose a … well … one of those ……………… of film
3 They're connected to a ……………… for the sound, but I don't know the ……………… of that.

What might people like about watching films in these different situations?

Why do you think the people in these different groups are playing music?

6 In pairs, say how you could explain what you meant by these words if you forgot the name for them.

a cello   a documentary   a microphone   a scriptwriter

7 🔊 10 Listen to the last part of each conversation again and tick (✓) the phrases the candidates used to answer these questions.

In which of these situations would you like to watch a film? Which of the activities would you prefer to do?

I'd rather … ☐	I'd sooner … ☐
I'd definitely … ☐	I think it's better to … ☐
I'd prefer to … ☐	

✓ Exam task
Now you are each going to talk about two more pictures for one minute. Candidate A, turn to page 78 and Candidate B, turn to page 79. Ask your partner the question above the pictures and time him/her for one minute.

💡 Exam tip
If you don't know a word, use a phrase to explain it.

UNIT 3   25

Writing

Part 2 review
✏️ ›› Page 100

1 Work in pairs. Answer the questions below.

1 What is your favourite type of film? Tick (✓) the one(s) you like best.

> action films   animations   animé   cartoons
> comedies   coming-of-age   documentaries
> fantasy   horror films   romantic comedies (romcoms)
> science-fiction films   thrillers   westerns

2 What makes a film enjoyable? Tick (✓) the things you think are most important.

> animations   the acting   the casting
> the characters   the direction   the location
> the plot   the script   the sound track
> the special effects   the stunts

2 Read the exam task below and answer the questions.

1 Can you write about a comedy, thriller or horror film? Yes or no? Why?
2 Can you write a negative opinion of the film? Yes or no? Why?

✅ Exam task

Your English teacher has asked you to write a review for the film club website of a film in which the main character is a teenager. Describe the film and the main character. Say what happens in the film and explain whether you would recommend it to other people.

3 Read the model answer for the exam task below and answer the questions.

1 Does the review give a clear impression of the film and the main character?
2 Does it make you want to see the film? Why? / Why not?
3 What tense is used in the review? Could you use any other tense?

The Girl Who Leapt Through Time

This coming-of-age animé is one of my favourites, essentially because the main character, Konno Mokoto, is so relatable. **(1)** .... the story has fantasy elements, this character seems very real – many people my age would behave just like her if they were in her situation. The film takes you on a rollercoaster ride of emotions through many clever twists and turns in the story.

Mokoto is at a stage in her life when she's struggling to make decisions about her future. One day she discovers she can travel back in time. She uses this ability to fix minor things in her life, **(2)** .... getting better grades and having more fun with friends. **(3)** ...., she doesn't consider the consequences her actions have on others. Eventually, she realises she can't stay in the past forever, and she learns to make better choices.

This film is very powerful. The experiences of the main character teach us important lessons about the impact of decisions we make. It's **(4)** .... a great story about friendship. The animations, designed by Yoshiyuki Sadamoto, are excellent too. If you haven't seen this movie, put it at the top of your 'to-watch' list.

Writing

4 Read the review again and tick (✓) the correct box.

Where you find …	Paragraph 1	Paragraph 2	Paragraph 3
a description of what happens in the film			
the reviewer's recommendation			
a summary of the effect of the film			
what kind of film it is			

5 In pairs, find which of these elements are mentioned in the review. Then discuss what the reviewer thought of the elements mentioned and how you know this.

the plot   the main character   the soundtrack   the overall effect of the film
the direction   the animations   the type of film

6 Complete the gaps in the text with these linking words, with capital letters where necessary.

> also   although   however   such as

✓ Exam task

Choose one of the exam tasks below and write your review in **140–190** words.

1 You have seen this English-language advertisement in a magazine called *Film*.

> **Film reviews wanted! The best thriller ever.**
> Have you seen a really exciting thriller recently? Write a review telling us about it. You should include information about the plot, the action scenes and the characters, and tell us whether you would recommend the film.
> The best film reviews will be posted on our website next month.
> Write your **review**.

2 You have seen this announcement in an international magazine for teenagers.

> **Film reviews wanted! Comedies**
> Have you seen a really enjoyable comedy recently? Write a review telling us about the characters and what happens in the film, and say whether you would recommend the film to your friends.
> The best reviews will be published in our magazine next month.
> Write your **review**.

Remember to:
- make sure you give the name of the film.
- plan your writing with three paragraphs.
- try to use some colourful vocabulary.
- use some linking words/phrases.
- write 140–190 words (at least 170 words if you can).

UNIT 3

Grammar

Linking words
Page 84

1 The underlined linking words in these sentences are used incorrectly. Find examples in the text on page 22 where they are used correctly. Then correct the mistakes.

1 While the fact that we had a lot of food for dinner, I managed to eat it all.
2 On Fridays I play football. In spite of on Tuesdays I play tennis.
3 I go running in the morning. Although I don't like running in the evening.
4 However I had fun watching the game, I wouldn't say it was the best I'd been to.
5 I went shopping with my sister in spite of I don't like shopping myself.
6 Even though making some tasty meals, Alice was never taught to cook.

The passive
Page 84

2 Make the sentences passive.

1 Someone cleaned my bedroom while I was asleep!
2 You can find lots of bargains on this app.
3 Someone had given the school secretary my date of birth.
4 People think that protesters are to blame for the graffiti.
5 Someone has stolen my wallet!
6 They're changing the colour of all the classroom walls.
7 They will give you a camera to use on the film course.

3 Now write the verbs from Exercise 2 in the correct column in the table.

Tenses	Verb form	Past participle
present simple		
present continuous		
future simple		
past simple		
present perfect		
past perfect		
with modals		

4 Correct these mistakes made by exam candidates with the passive.

1 These days everything has been running by computers.
2 I was show a brochure which contained some exciting holiday destinations.
3 The club first founded in 1886.
4 Will food provide in the price of the school trip?
5 My mother called Naomi.
6 The show supposed to start at 6.00, but the actor was ill.
7 The park located in a beautiful part of London.
8 The museum tour arranged a month ago.
9 This cathedral has been builded in the early 14th century.
10 My parents have a holiday home that situated just one mile from the beach.

Reading and Use of English

Part 4

1 In Reading and Use of English Part 4 you have to complete a sentence using a prompt word so that it means the same as the original above it. You must write only two to five words in the gap. Look at the example below and the answer options A, B, C, D. Match them with the correct comment.

Tomorrow, my brother's got a job interview at the shoe factory.
BEING
Tomorrow, my brother ……………………………… a job at the shoe factory.

A will be interviewed for
B is being interviewed for
C intends being at an interview for
D will enjoy being interviewed for

1 This answer is right.
2 This answer has too many words.
3 This answer has the wrong meaning.
4 This answer doesn't use the prompt word.

2 Part 4 gaps usually require two main elements of grammar or vocabulary. Read the example below and answer the questions about it.

Everyone was disappointed when the head teacher cancelled the trip at the last moment.
WAS
To everyone's *disappointment, the trip was cancelled* by the head teacher at the last moment.

1 Why does *disappointed* need to change to *disappointment*?
2 Why does *cancelled* have to change to *was cancelled*?

3 Now read this example and answer the questions. Then write your answer in the gap.

The school concert should have finished before 9.00 but it went on until 10.00.
SUPPOSED
The school concert …………………………………………………………………… over by 9.00 but it went on until 10.00.

1 What word must you use in the gap?
2 Must *supposed* be a passive or an active form? Why?
3 After *supposed*, do you use the infinitive or *-ing* form of a verb?
4 What verb will go before *over*? Why?

Exam tip

If you have written more than five words you have made a mistake.

Exam task

For questions **1–6** complete the second sentence so that it has a similar meaning to the first sentence, using the word given. **Do not change the word given**. You must use between **two** and **five** words, including the word given.

1 Although Roberto was really tired, he managed to score a goal in the match.
SPITE
Roberto managed to score a goal in the match, ………………………… ………………………… really tired.

2 The school is going to build a new sports centre beside the music studio.
WILL
A new sports centre ………………………………………………… to the music studio.

3 Recording artists are critical of the pay they get from streaming services.
BY
Pay from streaming services ……………………………………………………… recording artists.

4 When Spanish Flamenco music begins, I immediately want to get up and dance.
AS
Spanish Flamenco music makes me want to dance …………………………… ………………………… starts.

5 The band expects to make the new album available before the tour next year.
RELEASED
The band's new album should ……………………………………………………… advance of the tour next year.

6 The orchestra has thought of something to attract larger audiences.
UP
The orchestra has ……………………………………………… way of attracting larger audiences.

4 Fit and healthy

SPORT

Reading and Use of English

1 In pairs, look at photo A above and discuss these questions.

1. What is this sport called in
   a) British English?
   b) American English?
2. Which man is the referee? What is the short form of 'referee'?
3. What do you think is happening in this interaction? Answer using these words: *tackle*, *opponent*.
4. How do you feel about this sport?

2 Look at photo B and read the nouns in the box below. Circle the nouns that you can see in the photo and underline two words that mean the same.

> court   defender   fault   goal scorer
> goalie   goalkeeper   pitch   referee
> shin guards   spectator   umpire

3 Look at the words that are not circled. Which sport are they from?

Part 5

4 Read the whole text, *Furia*, and answer the questions.

What type of text is this? How do you know?

A a novel   B a magazine article   C a blog

5 Read again and answer the questions.

1. How do we know Camila Hassan was rushing to the football field? Underline the text that tells us this.
2. How does the author tell the reader about Roxana's feelings?
   A by describing her emotions
   B by describing what she did

6 Answer this exam question.

On Camila's arrival at the Parque Yrigoyen field for football practice,

A she had to put her kit on quickly.
B a team mate was annoyed with her.
C the team left nowhere for her to stand.
D a referee was unhappy with her equipment.

7 Read questions 2 and 5. They are about how the main character, Camila, feels. Underline in the text the things Camila does and says that tell us the answers.

> 💡 **Exam tip**
>
> In Part 5 texts from novels, you often have to work out how people feel or what their attitude is from what they say and do, **not** from descriptions of their emotions.

Reading and Use of English

Exam task

You are going to read an extract from a text about a teenager from Argentina called Camila Hassan. For questions **1–5**, choose the answer (**A**, **B**, **C** or **D**) which you think fits best according to the text.

1 In the second paragraph, what happens in the interaction between Camila and Coach Alicia?
  A Camila tells Coach Alicia something that isn't true.
  B Camila responds to a look that Coach Alicia gives her.
  C Camila implies that Coach Alicia is treating her unfairly.
  D Camila uses her lack of kit as an excuse.

2 What do we learn about Camila in the third paragraph?
  A She struggles to have faith in her own potential.
  B She finds some of her coach's ideas amusing.
  C She wishes her coach would stop exaggerating.
  D She is determined to become a top footballer.

3 How does Camila feel about her brother, Pablo?
  A She is envious of the fact it is easy for him to play football.
  B She would like to be as skilled a player as he is.
  C She dislikes how motivated he is by money.
  D She is concerned that he is too ambitious.

4 What point does Coach Alicia make about Pablo?
  A His career as a professional is likely to be short.
  B The fact that he is a professional has little significance.
  C Camila should try to follow him into professional football.
  D He has a disadvantage as a result of being a professional player.

5 How did Camila feel when she was given the captain's arm band?
  A She was proud to be chosen to lead the team.
  B She realised she couldn't let her doubts stop her.
  C She recognised that all her efforts were being rewarded.
  D She knew that she had to prove her physical fitness.

FURIA

The bus arrived in Bario General Jose de San Martin just as my watch pointed at three fifteen. I was late. I ran the rest of the way to Parque Yrigoyen field. Central Cordoba's stadium loomed right behind it, but our girls' league had no access there. When I arrived, a referee in antiquated black – a guy – was checking my team's shin guards. Roxana, our goalie and my best friend, sent me a killer glare as I peeled out of my sweatpants and sweater to reveal the blue and silver of my uniform. I took the last place in line and knocked on my shins to prove I was protected.

The rest of the girls dispersed and I laced my boots, Pablo's hand-me-downs, which were falling apart and smelt like an animal had died and decomposed in them.
'You're late Hassan,' Coach said. A lifetime of squinting and playing tough in a man's world had left a map of lines on her face, which said I'd better apologise or I wouldn't like my destination.
'I'm sorry.' I didn't promise it wouldn't happen again. I could lie to my mom but to Coach Alicia? Absolutely not.

On the opposite side of the field, the Royals in purple and gold warmed up, doing jumping jacks and stretches.
'Today is a big day,' Coach Alicia muttered like she was talking to herself, but I recognised the hope blazing in her words. If we won we'd go to the Sudamericano women's tournament in December, and that would bring us all kinds of things that were impossible right now. Exposure. Opportunities. Respect. I was a dreamer, but Coach Alicia was one of the most ambitious people I knew. She wanted so much for us.
'If we win, a pro team might finally notice you ... I had hoped Gabi would be here today, but in December? By then there'll be no hiding your talents, Hassan.'

Coach's sister Gabi worked with a super successful team somewhere up north. The rebellious *futboleras* like us couldn't go pro in Argentina. In the States, though, it was a different story. Every time Coach talked about some of us girls going pro, I wanted to believe her. But to hide my ridiculous dreams I laughed dismissively.

Coach Alicia pierced me with her falcon eyes. 'Don't laugh. You might not be playing at El Gigante yet but you have more talent than your brother. You'll go further than he will. Mark my words.'
Pablo would be richer for sure. I only wanted the chance to play, but even that was like wishing for the moon.
Coach Alicia half smiled. 'You have something Pablo doesn't.'
'What?'
'Freedom from society's expectations.'
'Thanks, I guess.'
'Now don't give me that look.' She placed an arm over my shoulder in an almost-hug.
'Pablo's a professional now. If he doesn't perform, the press slays him. You don't have that pressure, except from me. I want nothing but the best from you today. Esta claro?'
'Like water,' I replied, still wounded.
She winked at me and handed me a captain band. She walked away before I could explain that she was asking too much, that I was just a girl with strong legs and a stubborn streak. There is no time for drama, though. I wrapped the band around my arm and did a quick warm up on my own. Too soon, Coach called us in for a huddle. Sandwiched between Roxana and Cintia, I gazed at my team mates' faces as Coach Alicia urged us to leave everything we had on the pitch.

Listening

Part 2

1 Read the sentences about young skateboarders and answer these questions.

Into which gap or gaps must you put

1 a singular noun?
2 a plural noun?
3 a number?

> **Why are there so many brilliant young skateboarders?**
>
> 1 The youngest winning skateboarder at the Tokyo Olympics was .... years old.
> 2 At the Tokyo Olympics, the sport that the youngest athlete took part in was ....
> 3 The speaker says young skateboarders have less fear because they've had fewer .... than older skateboarders.
> 4 Another advantage of young skateboarders is that their .... is faster when they're learning.

2 Which gap in Exercise 1 could each of these words go in?

> 12   15   diving   injuries   memory   recovery   responsibilities   table tennis

3 🔊 11 Listen to the talk about young skateboarders. Choose the correct word from the box in Exercise 2 for each gap in Exercise 1.

✓ Exam task

In Listening Part 2 you will hear a long recording and answer ten questions on it. The task below has six questions.

🔊 12 You will hear part of a presentation about a young skateboarder called Sky Brown. For questions **1–6**, complete the sentences with a word or short phrase.

1 During her early childhood, Sky's home was in ....
2 Sky says she usually learns new skills from .... these days.
3 Sky entered her first skateboarding competition in the year ....
4 The name of the track that Sky recorded is ....
5 Sky usually .... before breakfast each morning.
6 Sky would like to provide .... to other children.

💡 Exam tip

You usually need to write one word but sometimes you will write two or three words. The word(s) you write should be exactly what you hear.

Speaking

Part 3
>> Page 114

1. Which of the above activities would you choose to get fit? Which would you choose to have fun? Discuss with a partner. For each one, think about:
   - how fit you need to be to do the activity and how easy it is to learn.
   - if you can do the activity with other people and how competitive it is.
   - if you would like to do the activity regularly.

2. Now change partners and do the exam task below. Your discussion should last for about three minutes. Time yourselves. Here are some useful expressions.

Asking your partner's opinion	Reacting to your partner
What do you think?	Do you think so?
What would you choose?	Really?
How about you?	It's not the same for me because …
Do you think it's best to … ?	I feel the same because …
Shall we start with … ?	

Exam task

Many students do sport at school. Here are some ideas for you to think about and a question for you to discuss.

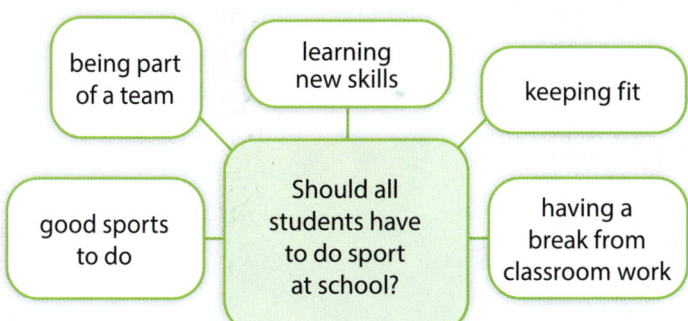

- being part of a team
- learning new skills
- keeping fit
- good sports to do
- having a break from classroom work
- Should all students have to do sport at school?

Now decide how often students should do sport at school each week.

Part 4
>> Page 116

3. In Speaking Part 4 you are asked for your opinions on a topic connected with Speaking Part 3, for example:

> Do you think people of your age do enough sport or do they prefer to watch TV?

Look at these opinions. Do you agree with any of them?

> It's much easier to watch TV or go on the computer than make an effort to do sport.

> It can be expensive to do sport because you have to pay for somewhere to play.

> Well, teenagers do watch a lot of TV but watching sport on TV encourages you to go and do it.

> I think the problem is that there aren't enough places to do sport.

Exam tip

The examiner will ask you several questions so the discussion lasts for four minutes. Don't worry if you can't think of more to say as there will be another question.

Exam task

Work in pairs to answer the questions.
- Should there be more opportunities to do different sports at school? Why? / Why not?
- Why are some sports less popular than others?
- How can people who don't like competitive sport be encouraged to get fit? Why is that a good idea?

UNIT 4 33

Reading and Use of English

HEALTH

Part 2

1. Work in pairs. In Reading and Use of English Part 2, most gaps have a grammar focus. You must write only one word in each gap, and it must be spelt correctly. Look at the sentences below and discuss why the answer given is not correct. Then write the correct answer.

Healthy eating habits

Incorrect answers	Correct answers
1 Eat regularly and try *hard* to miss any meals.	....
2 It may be better to have four or five small meals a day *rater* than three large ones.	....
3 Take time over your meal. *Must* not rush your food, and chew each mouthful well.	....
4 It is harder to eat when you are stressed or angry *as* when you are calm.	....
5 After you *are* eaten a meal, wait a while before doing any physical activity.	....
6 Make sure you leave a gap of at least two hours between a meal *and then* going to bed.	....

2. Part 2 gaps sometimes test phrases. Complete the following sentences with words from the box. Compare your answers with your partner's.

| account | addition | instead | long | order | well |

1. When you want a snack, have some fresh fruit .... of a biscuit or chocolate bar.
2. In .... to eating healthy food, drinking plenty of water is recommended.
3. Eating chips is fine as .... as you don't have them too often.
4. Doctors recommend eating lots of fresh vegetables on .... of the vitamins and minerals they contain.
5. Get involved in choosing the food you eat at home in .... to make sure you enjoy what you eat.
6. As .... as eating healthily, do some physical activity every day.

Exam task

For questions **1–8**, read the text below and think of the word which best fits each gap. Use only **one** word in each gap. There is an example at the beginning (**0**).

Exam tip

Read the text quickly first, then write the missing words in the gaps. When you have finished, read the whole text again. Check that the words you've written make sense.

Healthier takeaways

A single takeaway meal can easily push you over the recommended daily maximum amount **(0)** ....of.... salt, fat and sugar. That's probably because many takeaway meals **(1)** .... designed to be convenient and tasty **(2)** .... opposed to nutritious and healthy.

However, **(3)** .... are some healthier takeaway choices. For instance, from a burger restaurant, choose a regular, single meat burger **(4)** .... of getting a breaded or battered chicken or fish burger. Have the burger without mayonnaise or cheese, and get extra salad with it. **(5)** .... you love chips, always get the thicker ones since they absorb less fat. When it comes to pizzas, choose lower-fat toppings **(6)** .... as vegetables, ham and prawns. With pasta dishes, go for a sauce made with tomatoes or vegetables **(7)** .... than with cream. Another tip is to avoid anything **(8)** .... is deep fried in oil. When eating takeaway Chinese food, for example, the 'steamed' options are a healthier alternative to the deep-fried 'crispy' options.

Reading and Use of English

Part 3

Vocabulary – Word building (2)

3 Look at the words in the second column. Make a noun from each one and write the suffix in the last column.

Making nouns	Noun		Noun suffix
from adjectives:	SILENT	silence	t + ce
	UNHAPPY	………………	………………
from verbs:	COMPLETE	………………	………………
	CONSUME	(person) ………………	………………

> **Exam tip**
> You may need to add some extra letters or change some letters before you add a suffix.

4 Make nouns from these words, using the suffixes from Exercise 3.

Adjectives: crazy   confident   lazy   convenient   friendly
Verbs: lecture   calculate   manufacture   associate   use   create

Exam task

For questions **1–8**, read the text below. Use the word given in capitals at the end of some of the lines to form a word that fits in the gap **in the same line**. There is an example at the beginning (**0**).

Sitting around all day doesn't make you happy!

It's well known that too much sitting increases the risk of (**0**) …*illnesses*… like heart disease, but a recent study found it can affect the mental health of teenagers too. (**1**) ……………… in the UK have collected data on 4,000 children from birth onwards, recording their physical (**2**) ……………… using tracking devices worn on the body. Each (**3**) ……………… in the study also answered a questionnaire which measured symptoms of depression such as low mood and poor (**4**) ………………. (**5**) ……………… of the data showed that between the ages of 12 and 16, time spent sitting increased by about 90 minutes a day, and depression scores became worse. Those who (**6**) ……………… spent large amounts of time seated had the worst depression scores.
However, the good news is that every hour of daily physical activity cuts the risk of depression by 10%. Every (**7**) ……………… hour further cut the risk. And the activity doesn't have to be doing sports; just doing everyday things like walking around at home more can make a (**8**) ……………….

ILL

RESEARCH

MOVE

PARTICIPATE

CONCENTRATE
ANALYSE

CONSTANT

ADDITION

DIFFERENT

Vocabulary – Health care

5 Make nouns (plural or singular) from these verbs and adjectives and complete the sentences with them. If you don't know the bolded words, look them up.

| addict | breathe | conscious | disabled |
| infect | injure | sick | treat |

1 The doctor asked Amal to take some deep ……………… while she listened to his **chest**.
2 Harry cut his finger and got a nasty ……………… in the **wound** that took ages to **heal**.
3 Nadya had such an ……………… to gaming that she rarely slept.
4 Taking plenty of rest is the best ……………… for a **virus** like flu.
5 Kyle **bumped** his head but didn't lose ……………….
6 People with ……………… may need extra help when using the gym equipment.
7 Juanita fell off her mountain bike but luckily didn't have any ……………….
8 Colds, stomach **bugs** and headaches are the most common ……………… at our school.

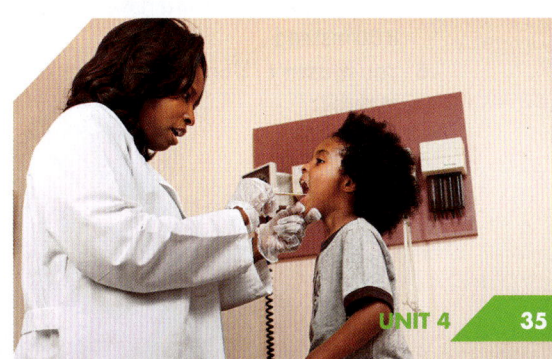

Grammar

Modal verbs
Page 85

1 Complete the sentences with one of the modal verbs given.

| can   can't   have to   should |

1 You .... feel more confident.
2 Unfortunately, they .... pick who they skate with.
3 The good news is they .... choose the music for their routine.
4 They .... follow the rules of the competition.

| could have lost   must have been rehearsing   should have been |

5 I .... picked for the team last year.
6 Last year's winner .... non-stop as his performance was even better this year.
7 We .... if we hadn't been at our best on the day.

2 Which sentence in Exercise 1 mentions something which:

a is allowed ....
b seems certain ....
c is advised ....
d isn't allowed ....
e was possible ....
f is a rule ....
g was expected ....

3 Now choose the correct verb in these sentences.

1 My family watch TV on the weekends when we **mustn't** / **don't have to** work.
2 She **must** / **had to** be quick because she was already late.
3 I don't remember the time but it **should** / **must** have been a Monday.
4 Every time Colin was late, his mother thought that something **must** / **should** have happened to him.
5 The bus **must** / **should** have left at 7.00 but it left at 8.00 instead.
6 You **mustn't** / **don't have to** behave like that in public.

Prepositions: *at, in, on*
Page 87

4 Tick (✓) the correct sentences. Correct the sentences with mistakes.

1 They waited patiently on the back door for him to come back.
2 They had to wait all afternoon at the queue for the opera tickets.
3 That snake is reputed to be the most poisonous on the world.
4 All the cutlery is on the tray ready to be carried into the dining room.
5 He used to own a luxury villa on the outskirts of that medieval town.
6 The facilities in that cruise ship are incredible.

5 Complete the sentences with the correct preposition.

1 In old spy films they often exchanged prisoners .... the border.
2 Over two hundred guests were .... the wedding reception.
3 He kept all his rubbish .... his attic rather than getting rid of it.
4 Their head office is .... a prestigious part of the capital.
5 The criminals who burgled my flat will be .... court tomorrow.
6 We played football all day .... the new pitch.

Writing

Part 2 email / letter
✎ ▶▶ Page 98

1 Read this exam question.

> You have received a letter from your English speaking pen friend.

> I start at my new school soon, and I discovered yesterday that we all have to do sport on Wednesday afternoons. As you know, I'm not that keen on sport, but at least I've got the choice of doing volleyball, tennis or athletics. Have you done any of these? Which is easiest? Which do you think I should choose?
>
> Write soon,
>
> Alex

With your partner discuss what advice you would give Alex. Use these phrases.

I'd advise/recommend him to …
I'd suggest/recommend … -ing
He could/should …

2 Read this reply. Put these phrases in the gaps, with capital letters where necessary.

| don't worry too much about | I suggest you | it should | it'd be better to |
| recommend doing | remember that | why not | you can |

> Hi Alex,
>
> The first thing I'd say is (1) ……………… having to do a sport. I know you've never been particularly sporty, but there'll be other people like you! Anyway, just (2) ……………… doing sport is a great way to make friends, so (3) ……………… turn out to be a positive experience in the end!
>
> I've played a lot of tennis, and learning all the different strokes takes a very long time. It's really difficult, so perhaps (4) ……………… do something else. Athletics can be fun, but a lot of the people who take it up are very serious, and go in for competitions and so on. For that reason, (5) ……………… avoid it.
>
> (6) ……………… take up volleyball? I'd (7) ……………… a team sport because you're bound to meet lots of people, which is a good thing when you're starting at a new school. Best of all, (8) ……………… have fun even if you don't play brilliantly. That's because compared to tennis and athletics, it really isn't difficult to learn. I often play volleyball with friends at the weekend, and in the summer we occasionally play on the beach.
>
> Good luck with everything – and let me know how it goes!
>
> Pete

3 Read Pete's letter again. Are these sentences true or false?

1 He begins his letter with some general advice.
2 He talks about two of the three sports Alex mentions.
3 He doesn't give reasons for the advice he gives.
4 He talks about his own experience of sport.
5 He finishes his letter by repeating his advice.
6 He has written in an appropriate style.

💡 **Exam tip**

Make sure you know phrases to express language functions like recommending things, asking for and giving advice, and suggesting ideas to people.

✅ **Exam task**

4 Read the email below with your partner, and decide what advice you could give to Sam.

5 Write an answer to the email.

> You have received an email from your English-speaking friend.

Remember to:
- make sure you understand the whole situation.
- plan your letter or email before you begin.
- write in an appropriate style.
- begin and end appropriately.
- write 140–190 words.

> Help! I've got a difficult decision to make. I've just got into my school football team, so there'll be lots of matches to play on a Saturday. But I've also just got a place in a local orchestra for young people, and all the concerts they do are also on a Saturday. I can't do both, so which shall I choose?
>
> Write soon.
>
> Best wishes, Sam

Write your **email**.

UNIT 4 37

5 Lessons learnt

ACHIEVEMENTS

Reading and Use of English

1 Look at these photos. Which one is a sports coach, a code writer, a gardener and a construction worker?

2 In pairs, read the table suggesting how necessary some personal qualities are. Discuss how far you agree with it, and why.

What qualities does a gardener need?	Essential	Helpful	Not necessary
physical strength	✓		
creativity		✓	
wisdom			✓
honesty		✓	
politeness		✓	
enthusiasm	✓		
courage			✓
willingness to learn	✓		
the capacity to inspire others			✓
understanding of others			✓

3 Now discuss which columns in the table should be ticked for the other three jobs.

4 Match the definitions with a quality from the table in Exercise 2. In pairs, compare your answers.

1 the ability to deal with a dangerous or difficult situation without being frightened ....
2 the tendency to tell the truth ....
3 having a strong body ....
4 the ability to influence others ....
5 having a deep understanding of the world ....
6 having good manners ....
7 the desire to acquire new knowledge and skills ....
8 the ability to sympathise with how people feel and think ....
9 being artistic and having original ideas ....
10 a quality of eagerness in your approach to something ....

Part 7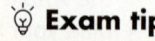

💡 Exam tip

Read text A, go through the questions and find all the A answers. Repeat for texts B–D. Finally, go back and look for any missing answers.

Reading and Use of English

Exam task

You are going to read a magazine article about teenagers who did some volunteer work in the holidays. For questions **1–10**, choose from the people (**A–D**). The people may be chosen more than once.

Which person

says that all the volunteers felt united by the aim of the project?	1
mentions a financial motivation for his project using volunteers?	2
says he expects what he learnt on the project to be valuable in his professional life?	3
mentions the effect of his personality on the people he was working with?	4
describes the healthier habits he had during his time as a volunteer?	5
says he began to realise the difficulty involved in a certain profession?	6
says he particularly liked encouraging participation?	7
admits he wanted something that was not available to him while volunteering?	8
explains why he was so well suited to the project?	9
admits he didn't always enjoy his time on the project?	10

Teenage Volunteers

Here four young people describe how they spent their holidays helping other communities

A Sven, 14 years old

I've just returned from volunteering in Swaziland with an organisation called Kaya, which arranges volunteer opportunities around the world for young people. I worked on a local project which has successfully introduced sports into the curriculum of seven community nursery schools. Without the project these children would not be able to access sports activities, so would miss out on opportunities to develop physical skills as well as important interpersonal skills such as team working and listening to others. I was impressed at the children's willingness to learn how to do the activities, which ranged from gymnastics to horse riding. I've always loved doing sports, in fact I find it hard to sit still, so this was the ideal role for me. I got to do a wide variety of activities with the kids every day, and I think my energy and enthusiasm inspired the children to have a go at new activities. The highlights of my time there were the times I succeeded in getting the shy children to join in and have fun.

B Mehmet, 19 years old

I've just spent two weeks in northern England, living in a large tent with four strangers from across the world. The four of us, aged 18–35, were volunteers giving our time and energy to help build an eco-friendly house for an English family. To make the building of their ambitious new home affordable, the family invites volunteers to help them out in return for accommodation, meals and training in green building skills. Although at times the work seemed tough and unpleasant, after each day of construction it was rewarding to see the progress we'd made and then have some fun together. It was a great way to get out of my comfort zone, gain a better understanding of a green lifestyle, make new friends, have fun, and help others in the process!

C Matteo, 13 years old

Last summer, my mum and I volunteered on a project in South Africa. It brought together people of all ages and nationalities who developed a bond through a common goal: to restore the natural environment in a region which had been severely damaged by fire a few years previously. The organisers called the project a festival, and that's what it felt like, despite the hours of hard work we did. We were mainly involved in tree planting and removal of invasive plant species, and each evening the organisers put on music, dancing and wonderful meals. I'm afraid I did miss being able to get fast food, but the nutritious diet and no sugary drinks, plus daily physical work meant I came home much fitter. I also picked up a lot of information on environmental issues as a result of conversations with the project leaders and the volunteers who were university students.

D David, 18 years old

I recently took part in a volunteering project run by students at my university. Student volunteers gave their time for free to deliver two weeks of computer coding sessions to children from local schools during the summer holidays. What I found rewarding was the fact that, by the end of the two weeks, we could see clearly the product of our teaching: delighted children confidently writing code for an app. The project also gave me the opportunity to develop skills such as organisational and communication skills, all of which will be beneficial in any future career I may choose. Another lesson I learnt was just how much courage and creativity teachers need, especially with larger groups. But the results you get more than make up for any struggle. I'd recommend this project to any student.

Listening

1 Work in pairs. Look at the photos below of outdoor areas at schools. Discuss the following questions.

1. What are the children doing in each photo?
2. What educational value do each of the areas have for students?
3. Which one would you like to spend time in during school time? Why?

Part 2

2 Read these Listening Part 2 sentences and answer options. For each sentence, cross out one answer which is not possible. Tell a partner why it is not possible.

The School Farm

1. At Castle School farm, they grow **aubergines** / **cherries** / **prawns** inside a greenhouse.
2. The only animals the school farm has are **goats** / **beef** / **chickens**.
3. The farm was set up in order to give students **social** / **musical** / **practical** skills.

3 🔊 13 Now listen to a teacher talking about a small farm at his school. Choose the correct answers in Exercise 2. Note that you will hear both of the two possible answers remaining, so choose your answers carefully.

💡 Exam tips

- You hear words which mean the same as the sentences, but they're not exactly the same words.
- Some words you hear could fit in the gaps but are not correct, so listen carefully to the meaning of each part of the recording.

✓ Exam task

🔊 14 You will hear a student called Katya giving a presentation at a school council meeting about improving their school's outdoor area. For questions **1–10**, complete the sentences with a word or short phrase.

Improving our outdoor area: ideas from four other schools

The skatepark at Prince's School was built where the students used to play **(1)** ....
Skateboarding **(2)** .... are held in the skatepark at Prince's School.
In The Kite School wildlife garden, students planted wild flowers to bring **(3)** .... into it.
Creatures like birds and a fox have visited the **(4)** .... in the wildlife garden.
In the future, students are going to put a **(5)** .... in their wildlife garden.
Tower Road School built a beach as somewhere for students to **(6)** ....
The wall around the beach has a picture of a **(7)** .... on it.
Low Beck School outdoor theatre was built and **(8)** .... by parents at the school.
From their theatre seats, audiences can see the **(9)** .... that surround Low Beck School.
In the summer, there are **(10)** .... and drama productions at the outdoor theatre.

Grammar

Conditionals
>> Page 87

a  b  c

1 Complete these conditional sentences.

1 If I weren't revising for important exams, I ………………………… more of my time relaxing.
2 If they had stopped me from going, I ………………………… that I love writing poetry.
3 If I want to succeed, I ………………………… work extremely hard.
4 If you want to do well in any career, you ………………………… build up a good reputation.

2 Which sentence in Exercise 1 is about:

a past events which can't be changed?
b something which is likely in the future?
c something which is impossible or unlikely?
d something which is a general statement of fact?

3 Read the examples and then complete the definitions below with the underlined expressions.

> You can go out with your friends <u>providing (that) / provided (that)</u> you finish your housework.
> James will come swimming <u>as/so long as</u> he finishes his homework in time.
> Should I bring my umbrella <u>in case</u> it rains?
> We can go to the beach <u>unless</u> it rains.

1 ………………………… means because it's possible something might happen.
2 ………………………… means the same as *except if*.
3 ………………………… and ………………………… mean the same as *only if* or *on condition that*.

4 Choose the correct expression in these sentences.

1 I'd suggest you take some money with you **unless** / **in case** you want to buy anything.
2 I won't watch the film **if** / **unless** there's a game on TV I want to watch.
3 I'll lend you some money **in case** / **so long as** you promise to pay me back.
4 I'll meet you tomorrow **unless** / **as long as** you let me know you can't come.

UNIT 5 | 41

Reading and Use of English

EDUCATION

Part 1

Vocabulary – Phrasal verbs

1 In Reading and Use of English Part 1, you often need to know phrasal verbs. Look back at the texts on page 39 and find the words which complete these phrasal verbs.

Text A: miss .... join ....
Text B: help ....
Text C: put .... pick ....
Text D: make ....

2 When choosing a phrasal verb, it's very important to read the text after the gap carefully as well as before it. Choose the correct ending to follow the phrasal verbs.

1 Sarah didn't go to the lesson so she missed out on
  a a hot, difficult afternoon.
  b a chance to revise for the exam.

2 Katie offered to help Henri out
  a with his chores.
  b but he was tired.

3 The lovely dinner Dad cooked made up for
  a the awful day we'd had.
  b the wonderful trip we went on.

4 At the end of term, the school usually puts on
  a the director of the play.
  b a concert in the local theatre.

5 When Finn stayed with his penfriend in France, he picked up
  a French lessons every day.
  b quite a lot of French vocabulary.

6 In big groups, shy people find it hard to join in
  a with discussions that take place.
  b because it's easier for them.

> **Exam tip**
>
> Make sure the word you choose has a meaning that fits the text after the gap as well as before it.

Exam task

For questions **1–8**, read the text below and decide which answer (**A, B, C** or **D**) best fits each gap. There is an example at the beginning (**0**).

The Youth Leadership & Community Service online programme

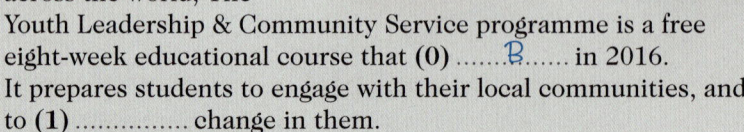

Designed to connect hundreds of young people across the world, The Youth Leadership & Community Service programme is a free eight-week educational course that (0) ...B... in 2016. It prepares students to engage with their local communities, and to (1) .... change in them.

It's (2) .... to teenagers aged 14 to 19 who have basic English language (3) .... and can devote four hours weekly to the programme.

Using digital platforms like Canvas, Padlet and Zoom, participants take part in group projects and (4) .... activities like asking a community project leader questions during a live webinar. Participants also (5) .... friendships worldwide through small-group video calls, learning as much from one another as from programme facilitators.

Leadership and product-design skills are taught through webinars and workshops to (6) .... participants to plan their own projects. On (7) .... of the course, participants receive a leadership certificate and many successfully (8) .... out the plans that they've come up with during the programme.

0	A presented	B launched	C introduced	D departed
1	A come across	B put out	C bring about	D take off
2	A public	B allowed	C possible	D open
3	A condition	B cleverness	C competence	D capacity
4	A functional	B interactive	C effective	D involved
5	A form	B construct	C raise	D produce
6	A fulfil	B enable	C authorise	D realise
7	A completion	B ending	C achievement	D closure
8	A keep	B put	C carry	D make

Reading and Use of English

Part 4

3 Some Reading and Use of English Part 4 tasks mainly require a vocabulary change. Read the examples below and say which one requires a change in the main vocabulary.

1 I suddenly thought of how I could persuade my mum to let me go on the trip.
   CAME
   I suddenly *came up with a way of* persuading my mum to let me go on the trip.

2 I won't be chosen for the team if I don't practise enough.
   UNLESS
   I won't be chosen for the team *unless I practise* more.

4 Match the phrases with the same meaning. In pairs, check your answers.

1 look forward to something
2 take part in something
3 go ahead with something
4 come across something
5 get on well with someone
6 catch up with someone
7 fall out with someone

a start to do something
b hear someone's news
c can't wait for something to happen
d participate in something
e have a disagreement with someone
f find something unexpectedly
g be really friendly with someone

5 Complete the sentences using a phrase from Exercise 4, changing the grammar to match the first sentence.

1 Julien is really friendly with Gary.
   Julien .... with Gary.
2 Franz and Kylie fell out on Friday, and haven't spoken since.
   Franz and Kylie .... on Friday and haven't spoken since.
3 Over 200 students have taken part in this musical festival.
   Over 200 students .... in this musical festival.
4 Construction of the skatepark will start next Monday.
   Construction of the skatepark .... next Monday.
5 Sky always enjoys hearing her friends' news.
   Sky always enjoys .... her friends.
6 My parents can't wait to move house.
   My parents .... house.
7 Jamie found his wallet while looking for his phone.
   Jamie .... his wallet while looking for his phone.

Exam task

For questions **1–6**, complete the second sentence so it has a similar meaning to the first sentence, using the word given. **Do not change the word given.** You must use between **two** and **five** words, including the word given.

Exam tip

Think about whether the gap has a grammatical focus (for example, conditionals) or a vocabulary one (for example, phrasal verbs).

0 I'll come to the cinema if you let my sister come too.
   PROVIDED
   I'll come to the cinema *provided that my sister is* allowed to come too.

1 Ellie only took the train because her dad couldn't give her a lift.
   HAVE
   If Ellie's dad had been able to give her a lift, she .... by train.

2 In the park each summer, the orchestra holds concerts for kids.
   PUT
   In the park each summer, concerts .... by the orchestra for kids.

3 Uri will only go to the party if Sam goes too.
   LONG
   Uri will go to the party .... going too.

4 Book your place on the trip to make sure you get to see the amazing Silver Waterfalls!
   OUT
   Book your place on the trip so you don't .... the amazing Silver Waterfalls!

5 At the museum, there are lots of displays that visitors can interact with.
   MANY
   The museum .... displays for visitors.

6 Josh Harris won the Best Maths Student prize.
   AWARDED
   The prize for Best Maths Student .... Josh Harris.

UNIT 5   43

Speaking

Vocabulary – School subjects

1 Tick (✓) the subjects you are studying, then compare with a partner.

English	other foreign languages
my own language and literature	maths
science	history
geography	IT
sport	art
music	drama

other subjects: ……………………………………………

2 Tell your partner which of the subjects in Exercise 1 you like best. Use reasons a–e to explain why.

a I'm good at it.
b The teacher's great.
c It's an interesting subject.
d It'll be useful.
e Other: ……………………………………

Part 1
>> Page 108

3 Match the speech bubbles with the questions, then, in pairs, ask and answer them. Remember to add some extra information.

A I'd love to learn coding if I could.
B I hope to pass all my exams and go to university.
C I'd like to be a scientist if I get good grades.
D How to sit still!

Ambitions and achievements
1 What job would you like to do when you grow up?
2 What do you expect to achieve in the next five years?

Education
3 What was the most important thing you learnt at primary school?
4 Is there a new subject you'd really like to study?

Part 2
>> Page 110

4 Work in pairs and do the task below.

Candidate A: Look at photographs 1 and 2. Compare them and answer the question. Tell your answer to Candidate B. Use these phrases if you are not sure about what you see in the photos: *it may/might/could be a … it looks like a … it's similar to a … it's a sort of …*

Candidate B: When Candidate A has finished, discuss together which lesson you would prefer to do and why. Give reasons. Here are some phrases you can use: *I'd rather … because it's more interesting. It's good to learn something new. I'd rather be outside. I don't like/enjoy doing … because …*

💡 Exam tip

Don't worry if you don't know a particular word, or if you are unsure what you can see in the photographs! Keep talking and make intelligent guesses using the phrases above.

✓ Exam task

Now do the same with photographs 3 and 4 on page 80. Candidate B should start. Use the phrases in Exercise 4 to help you. When Candidate B has finished, discuss which of the visits you would prefer to go on and why.

What might pupils learn by doing these different subjects at school?

Writing

Part 2 article
>> Page 102

1 You may be asked to write an article about a topic that's familiar to many people. Your article can be quite informal, but you need to get the reader's attention and keep it. Tick (✓) the four strategies below that will most help you to do this.

1 making points as clearly as possible
2 describing everything in great detail
3 finishing in an interesting way
4 using long, very unusual words
5 making amusing comments
6 mentioning emotional responses to experiences

2 Read this task and the article that was written for it. Find examples of the helpful strategies in Exercise 1. Highlight them in different colours.

> You have seen this announcement on an international website:
>
> **Articles wanted!**
> The best school trip
> Have you ever been on a great school trip? Write and tell us where you went and why it was so good.
> The best articles will be posted on the website next month.
>
> Write your **article** in **140–190** words.

The best school trip I've ever been on

I have to admit I've only been on two school trips, so it's not hard for me to choose which one was best! It was a day trip to Garrs Forest with my class last year.

There are many reasons why this trip was so good. But (1) ...., the forest ranger who led our group was brilliant. She was fairly tall, had black curly hair and wore a smart green ranger's uniform. She took us for a walk through the forest, and showed us loads of plants, bugs and mushrooms I'd never have spotted without her. We were (2) .... taken to a beautiful place deep in the forest, where we were asked to sit without speaking for three minutes. (3) .... my friend Jordi kept quiet, which is extremely unusual! We all felt really calm afterwards.

Next, we had lunch in the visitor centre, and then the ranger gave us a fun quiz. We had to guess whether some amazing facts about forests were true or false. (4) ...., trees can communicate underground through fungi roots called mycelium. It's true!
I'll always remember that trip, and it taught me a lot. (5) ...., I think I learnt more that day than in a month at school!

3 The article is a bit too long. Which sentence would you cut? Why?

4 Write the following phrases in the gaps, with capital letters where necessary.

> also   even   for instance   in fact
> most importantly

5 Write a different beginning and ending for the article.

✓ Exam task

For homework, either answer the exam task in Exercise 2, or this one:

> Your English teacher has asked you to write an article for the school magazine with the title:
> *The best thing I've ever learnt from the internet*
> Write your **article** in **140–190** words.

Remember to:
• begin with an interesting introduction.
• express your points clearly.
• use past tenses and write in paragraphs.
• end in an interesting way.

UNIT 5

6 Our planet

Listening

1 In pairs, look at the footprint illustration which shows what creates your carbon footprint. Say which picture within the footprint represents:

> doing the laundry   electricity   fossil fuels
> heating and cooling systems   meat-based diets
> single-use plastic   transport   waste

2 Read the text. Write these words in the correct gaps.

> carbon emissions   carbon footprint   climate change
> global warming   greenhouse gas

A **(1)** .... is the total amount of carbon dioxide released into the atmosphere as a result of the activities of a particular individual, organisation or community.

Carbon dioxide is a **(2)** .... This means it traps the sun's heat in the Earth's atmosphere. This causes **(3)** .... , which ultimately leads to **(4)** ....

Nearly everything you do releases some amount of carbon into the atmosphere, but you can increase or decrease these **(5)** .... with your everyday choices.

3 Discuss which thing in each of these pairs is better for reducing your carbon footprint. Which picture in the diagram on the left represents it?

1. eating a vegan diet / eating a meat-based diet
2. petrol cars / electric cars
3. drying clothes on a washing line / drying clothes in a tumble drier
4. power from coal / wind power
5. solar panels / gas boilers
6. single-use plastic / recyclable plastic
7. flying / taking the train
8. saving energy / wasting energy

4 In pairs, tell each other how you try to reduce your carbon footprint, and say whether you think you do enough or you could do more.

Listening

Part 4

5 In Listening Part 4, you hear words that signal the topic for each question, and they are the same or very similar to words in the question. They help to keep you at the right place in the task.

🔊 **15** Listen and underline the word or words in the questions that signal each new topic in the recording.

Your carbon footprint

1 What does the speaker say about working out your carbon footprint?
2 The speaker thinks that eating organic food …
3 Regarding eating meat, what does the speaker recommend?

6 Now your teacher will show you the script. In pairs find the answers to the questions.

7 🔊 **16** Listen to the exam task recording, and focus on the question, not the answer options. Underline the words you hear that introduce the new topic, and are the same or very similar in the recording.

💡 Exam tips

- Listen for words that introduce the new topic for a question, and are the same or very similar words in the question. This helps you know where you are in the task.
- You hear the whole recording twice, so don't panic if you miss a question. Move on to the next question and do the missed question when you listen for the second time.

✓ Exam task

🔊 **16** You will hear an interview with a boy called Thomas who is talking about the environment club he started at his school. For questions **1–7**, choose the best answer (**A**, **B** or **C**).

1 The school visitor who inspired students and staff was
  A a business person.
  B a scientist.
  C a politician.

2 What change has happened as a result of the environment club's survey?
  A Students and teachers are creating a new transport plan together.
  B More students are coming to school on foot.
  C Fewer teachers drive their cars to the school.

3 What does Thomas say about the solar panels?
  A He was disappointed they couldn't get more of them.
  B He was keen to persuade others to install them elsewhere.
  C He was surprised at how quickly they could buy them.

4 What does Thomas regret about the tree planting?
  A upsetting some of the parents
  B having to change what was planned
  C losing space that was used for sports

5 How has recycling improved at the school?
  A Students know more about what materials can be recycled.
  B Students recycle more material where possible.
  C Students no longer mix up materials in the recycling bins.

6 What is Thomas's opinion about recycling?
  A Some approaches to it should be banned.
  B It's not the best way to reduce carbon use.
  C Many schools are doing little to promote it.

7 Thomas says the aim of the Environment Exhibition is to
  A collect new ideas for action at the school.
  B increase the membership of the environment club.
  C inspire other students to be more environmentally friendly.

8 Now your teacher will show you the script. In pairs, look at the recording script for each question, and underline the words that give you the answer.

UNIT 6 47

Speaking

Part 3
>> Page 114

1. Your school is thinking of things students can do to improve and protect the environment. Look at the suggestions below. Make some notes. For each suggestion think about:
   - what you could do in your school.
   - how successful it might be.

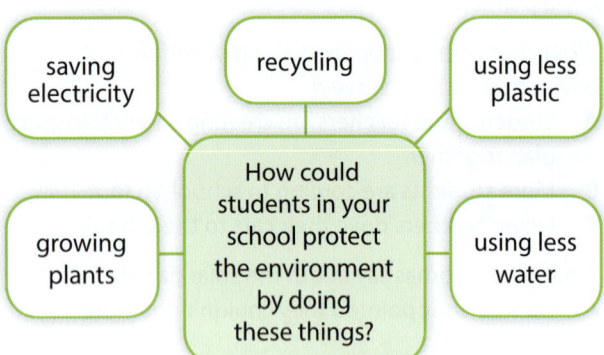

2. In Speaking Part 3, the examiner gives you a task with a question and some suggestions. You have a discussion about the suggestions and then you are asked to make a decision. Here are some useful expressions. Write A, D, C or S next to each one for Agree, Disagree, make a Comment, make a Suggestion.

   1. I don't really think that's a good idea.
   2. Absolutely.
   3. We all know we shouldn't drop litter.
   4. We could tell everyone to turn off their computers at the end of the lesson.
   5. I don't think turning the heating down would go down well with students here.
   6. I'm with you on that.
   7. That's not what I think, I'm afraid.
   8. What about getting recycling bins in the canteen?

Exam task

Now practise doing the task in Exercise 1 with your partner.
- Talk about the question and the suggestions for about two minutes.
- Which two suggestions would be most successful?

Exam tip

Start speaking straight away so you use the time allowed. Cooperate with your partner and ask him/her to respond, e.g. *What do you think? Do you agree? And you?*

Part 4
>> Page 116

Exam task

The examiner will ask you some general questions related to Part 3. You have four minutes to complete Part 4 in the exam. Take it in turns to ask and answer the questions below with your partner.

- Do you think your school is environmentally friendly? Why? / Why not?
- Do you think young people care about the environment more than older people? Why? / Why not?
- Are young people taught enough about the environment at school? Should there be any changes?
- Does the media do enough to make young people aware of environmental problems?
- Do people use cars too much instead of walking or cycling? Why is this a problem?

Writing

Part 2 review
>> Page 100

1 In pairs, look at the photos and discuss how bad you think these items are for the environment. Suggest alternatives to them that are more environmentally friendly. You can use the words in the box in your explanations.

verbs	adjectives
re-use	single-use
recycle	re-usable
throw away	greener
harm	durable
pollute	non-recyclable
	biodegradable

2 Look at the exam task below. What three things must your review include?

....

✓ Exam task

Write your answer in **140–190** words in an appropriate style.

You see this advert in an environmental magazine for teenagers:

Buy second hand and help the environment!
Second-hand shops

reviews wanted

Write a review of a second-hand shop that you know. The review should include information about what the shop sells, customer service in the shop, and whether you would recommend the shop to other people your age. The best review will be published in next month's magazine.

Write your **review**.

3 Now read the review. It's too short. What information has the writer missed out? Work with a partner and add the missing information.

My favourite second-hand shop

There is a great second-hand bookshop in my town called Re-readers. It sells all kinds of books, from children's storybooks to academic books for university students. When I was younger, I used to get children's storybooks from there, but more recently, I've bought some biology and physics text books for school. Everything I've bought there has been in really good condition, despite being second hand. I would definitely recommend this shop not just to people my age, but everyone. Second-hand books are just as good as new ones, and it's better for the environment to re-use things like books rather than throwing them away. They are also cheaper, which is another good reason to buy from this shop.

4 Now do this exam task.

✓ Exam task

Write your answer in **140–190** words in an appropriate style.

You see this advert in an environmental magazine for teenagers:

Green products used by teenagers

Reviews wanted

Write a review of a product you have bought that is environmentally friendly, such as a bamboo toothbrush, a re-usable drinks bottle or a cotton shopping bag. Your review should say where you can get the product, why it is environmentally friendly, and whether you would recommend this product to other people your age.

The best review will be published in next month's magazine.

UNIT 6 49

Reading and Use of English

WILDLIFE

1 Work in pairs. Look at the photos and names of wild animals. Can you identify each animal in the photos?

crab   crocodile   deer   eagle   owl   seal
swan   wasp   wolf   worm   zebra

2 In pairs, ask and answer these questions about the wild animals from the box in Exercise 1.

1 Which animals have wings?
2 Which animals hunt at night?
3 Which animal lives in soil?
4 Which animals have stripes?
5 Which animal has a shell?
6 Which animal lives only in a coastal habitat?
7 Which animals have more than four legs?
8 Which animals are indigenous to your country?

Part 6

3 In Reading and Use of English Part 6, the text after the gap is often most helpful in choosing the answer. In pairs, discuss what could go before each of these sentences.

1 But more often, the sea is really rough at this time of year.
2 This came as a surprise to most of the researchers.
3 It was also decided that students should design the wildlife garden themselves.
4 Plus, they attract pollinating insects like bees to the area.
5 If you prefer birds to insects, do your project on them instead.
6 This allows wild animals to cross the road safely.

4 Match these words and phrases in the exam task with their meanings.

1 data   5 conservation
2 reptile   6 endangered
3 species   7 record
4 observe   8 drought

a watch something carefully for a reason
b a long period when there is no rain
c at risk of becoming extinct
d the protection of nature
e to write down information or store it on a computer so that it can be used in the future
f a group of plants or animals which share similar characteristics
g a type of animal that produces eggs and uses the heat of the sun to keep its blood warm
h information or facts about something

💡 Exam tip

Read the text after each gap carefully, and work out what sort of information is needed in the gap before it. Then read the answer options.

✓ Exam task

You are going to read an article about citizen science in wildlife conservation. Six sentences have been removed from the article. Choose from the sentences **A–G** the one which fits each gap (**1–6**). There is one extra sentence that you do not need to use.

A In all, they discovered 119 different species growing in the pavements and walls.
B One, for example, involves searching a coastal area for hundreds of different species of seaweed.
C The most obvious one is the satisfaction they get from doing something useful for the world.
D The conservationists running the project interpreted the data.
E Even more importantly, they need to monitor how these factors change over time.
F Occasionally, specialist knowledge is required of them.
G Greater numbers were recorded on those in urban sites.

50

Reading and Use of English

SEARCH

Citizen scientists help wildlife conservation

Imagine discovering a new species of insect. You probably think you'd need to be an expert with all the latest equipment to do this, but that's not true. A few years ago, citizen scientists found 30 previously unknown fly species in Los Angeles.

Citizen science is scientific research carried out by amateurs, usually under the direction of professional scientists. It relies on ordinary adults, teenagers and even children to collect data. In the sphere of wildlife conservation, it's very hard to protect a species if little is known about it. To understand what a species needs, conservationists have to gather as much information as possible about the size of its population, its habitat choices and its behaviour.
(**1**) .... This allows conservationists to detect any abnormal trends that may be worrying.

However, conservationists alone would struggle to collect as much data as they need. That's where the citizen scientists come in. (**2**) .... But more often, all you need to get involved is a basic understanding of the subject area being studied. The project organisers may also provide a species-identification guide and offer you some training. When you spot an example of the target species, you are usually asked to take a photo of it and email it or upload that onto an app, together with some key details about it.

If you are interested in becoming a citizen scientist on a local wildlife conservation project, there is a wide range to choose from. (**3**) .... If you prefer animals to plants, there's a project that asks volunteers to look for the reptiles that are indigenous to a region.

Over the past few years, there have been some useful results from projects like these. In one, 30,000 school children from 400 schools across the UK counted how many bees they saw on lavender plants that were placed in a variety of city and countryside locations. (**4**) .... This came as a surprise to scientists, who will use the data supplied by the children to protect endangered populations of bees.

Another project in France involved hundreds of people investigating the wild flowers that lived in the streets of Paris. (**5**) .... It was also found that city plants are more tolerant of drought and pollution, and their seeds are spread by the wind rather than by insects or animals.

People who become citizen scientists say that being involved in wildlife conservation in this way has many benefits.
(**6**) .... Plus, children and teenagers can put their natural curiosity to good use, while learning how enjoyable and rewarding scientific research can be. Most adults find they start to look at their environment in a new way, often with greater interest and a wider understanding of their environment and the wildlife that lives in it.

---

5 Work in pairs to discuss the following.

1 When you have finished the task, compare your answers with a partner. If you disagree on an answer, look at the question again, and see if you can work out who is right.
2 What will you do in the exam if you are unable to answer a question?
3 Have you ever been a citizen scientist? If so, what did you do? If not, would you like to be one?

Countable and uncountable nouns
>> Page 89

1 *Scientist* is a countable noun and *wildlife* is an uncountable noun. Answer these questions about countable and uncountable nouns.
  1 Which kind of noun can be singular or plural?
  2 Which kind of noun cannot be plural and takes a singular verb?

2 Look back at the text and find three examples of countable and uncountable nouns.

Countable: ....
Uncountable: ....

UNIT 6 51

Grammar

Articles
>> Page 90

3 Complete the rules about articles with these words.

> a   an   no article   the

We use …

1 .... or .... with singular countable nouns that introduce a new item of information.
2 .... with countable and uncountable nouns, when the item has been mentioned before.
3 .... + noun when the speaker and listener both know what they are talking about.
4 .... with uncountable and plural countable nouns when we talk about things in a general sense.
5 .... with the names of most buildings, cities, countries, lakes, towns, villages and mountains.
6 .... with the names of certain countries (with the word *Kingdom*, *Republic* or *State*), regions, deserts, mountain ranges, oceans, rivers and seas.

4 Which of these place names need *the* before them? Write them next to the correct heading.

> Amazon   Atlantic Ocean   California
> Czech Republic   Far East   Himalayas   Italy
> Lake Como   London   north of England
> Sahara   South America   Thames
> United Kingdom   United States

Oceans, seas and rivers: the ....
Regions: the ....
Countries: the ....
Deserts and mountain ranges: the ....

Add some more examples to the lists if you can.

5 Complete these sentences with *a* or *the*.

1 I found .... cat downstairs in .... kitchen.
2 Barry asked for .... glass of water with ice but we had no ice left in .... freezer.
3 I enjoyed reading .... book you lent me. Is it part of .... series?
4 I've been memorising .... words for .... play.
5 I started watching .... TV show yesterday and it's .... best thing I've seen in months.

6 Which sentences need *the* and which need no article? Complete them with *the* or leave a gap.

1 Pupils at my school can decide whether they want to study .... history.
2 We learnt about .... history of making olive oil in class last week.
3 I asked my brother to give me .... money he owed me.
4 We want to raise .... money for the animal charity.

So and such (a/an)
>> Page 91

7 Complete the sentences with *so* or *such*.

1 The pupils reacted .... positively to the prospect of 'adopting' a class pet that the teacher arranged it at once.
2 The school trip to the zoo received .... a good response that they decided to make it an annual event.
3 Meerkats are .... shy animals that few people have seen one.
4 The antelope ran away .... quickly that the lion couldn't catch it.
5 The plans to build a new airport were dropped because .... many people reacted negatively towards it.
6 The trip to the safari was attended by .... a lot of people that there weren't enough seats on the bus.

8 Now complete the rules.

We use .... with nouns (with or without an adjective) and the expression *a lot* (*of*).

We use .... with an adjective or adverb and the words *many*, *much* and *few*.

Too and enough
>> Page 91

9 Look at the photo and complete the gaps in the sentence with *too* or *enough* and an adjective.

The first plant pot isn't .... , but the other one is ....

Reading and Use of English

Part 2

1 Match the typical Part 2 question focuses with examples of them.

Typical Part 2 question focuses	Examples
1 linking phrase	a has been, had gone, would have seen, didn't like
2 phrasal verb	b as many people as, more likely to work than, less easy to see than
3 pronoun	c the greatest number, the most peculiar
4 fixed phrase	d in spite of, in addition to, as long as
5 verb tense	e in front of, from, for, by, during
6 superlative form	f there will be, there have been, there probably weren't any
7 comparative form	g who, which, it, these, any
8 form of *there is/are*	h come up with, wake up, look down on, set off
9 preposition	i what on Earth, all over again, among other things, make a difference

2 Read the exam task and decide which of the question focuses from Exercise 1 is used in the example and the gaps.

✓ Exam task

For questions **1–8**, read the text below and think of the word which best fits each gap. Use only **one** word in each gap. There is an example at the beginning (**0**).

💡 Exam tip

Write your answers in the gaps, then read the text to make sure it makes sense before you transfer your answers to the answer sheet.

3 Check your answers with a partner. If you disagree, explain to each other why your answer is right or wrong.

Conservationists help the amur leopard

The amur leopard of eastern Russia and northern China is probably (**0**) ....*the*.... rarest big cat species on our planet. By the 1990s, they had (**1**) .... pushed almost to extinction by human activity. The leopards were being hunted (**2**) .... only for their beautiful coats, but also for their bones, to be used in traditional medicine. Furthermore, climate change, logging, forest fires and road building had destroyed huge areas of their habitat. (**3**) .... was thought that only about 30 individual amur leopards were left.

Happily, conservation programmes in the region have brought (**4**) .... significant improvement in amur leopard numbers (**5**) .... the beginning of this century. National parks have been created on both the Russian and Chinese sides of the border, (**6**) .... means that the leopards are protected from harmful human activity, and consequently now occupy a territory of about 2,350 square miles. Even (**7**) .... this is a positive change, the species remains classified as critically endangered because (**8**) .... are still only around 100 amur leopards in the wild.

7 Influences

BUYING AND SELLING

Reading and Use of English

1 Look at the two photos above and discuss what they are doing. Use these words.

> buying/selling   online/in-store
> consumer/entrepreneur

2 Look at the photos again, read the phrases and tick (✓) the correct column.

Who …	The seller	The buyer
is trying to make a profit?		
is making a living?		
is using a debit card?		
is purchasing something?		
is earning an income?		
is running a business?		
is making a payment?		
gets stock from suppliers?		
trades goods over the internet?		
is at the counter?		
might be getting a bargain?		

3 In pairs, answer these questions.

1 Do you like shopping? Why? / Why not?
2 If you like shopping, what kind of things do you like buying, and where do you buy them?
3 What are the advantages and disadvantages of buying these things?

> designer products   green products   imported goods
> sale items   top brands   vintage clothing

Part 5

4 Read the extracts from some articles and match them with what the writer is doing in the extract.

1 I tend to buy more second-hand clothes than any of my friends do.
2 The brands that Steffi makes most money from on her site are Cool Fox and Ranger.
3 I truly believe that today's teenagers are exceptionally entrepreneurial.
4 Choose your teen debit card provider carefully because some have hidden charges.
5 My parents prefer to shop locally. They only buy meat from the farm in our village, for instance.
6 Unfortunately, many teachers fail to see the talent that some teenage entrepreneurs have, and so these young people drop out of school.

a expressing an opinion   d identifying
b comparing   e complaining
c illustrating   f warning

> **Exam tip**
>
> In Reading and Use of English Part 5 questions that ask, *What is the writer doing … ?*, consider the first word of each option carefully because it is an important part of the answer.

5 Read the title and first paragraph of the article on the next page quickly. What is the article going to be about?

> **Exam task**

You are going to read an extract from an article about a teenage online-business owner. For questions **1–6**, choose the answer (**A**, **B**, **C** or **D**) which you think fits best according to the text.

Reading and Use of English

Jade Conti: twenty-first century entrepreneur

If you were born this century, the internet has always been part of the world you live in. This is likely to mean you have the ability to take advantage of all it has to offer, including new opportunities for getting rich – even if you're still at school! You can be an influencer, for example, creating online content to promote brands, or a seller of second-hand goods on auction sites. Or you could do what 15-year-old Jade Conti does. She makes money from buying new products and 'reselling' them at a higher price on various apps and websites that provide a marketplace for all kinds of sellers.

Last year, Jade resold £1.25 million worth of products through a handful of online marketplaces. Apart from packaging and delivery to customers, her only expense is a fee to the marketplace on each sale. To avoid paying rent on warehouse space, Jade keeps her stock in a barn on her uncle's farm. As a consequence of these factors, her profit of £92,000 for the year was higher than other business models would allow. With this amount in their pockets, many teenagers would spend like there's no tomorrow, but Jade's invested most of it back into her business.

Jade describes herself as 'kind of creative, and passionate about business', and these characteristics became evident at a very young age. Even though she's only 15 now, her business activities go back a couple of years before she became a reseller. To begin with, she sold toys she'd grown out of online, and when she had none left, began selling snacks to other kids at school.

Then Jade tried selling home-cooked biscuits, thinking that creating her own products would boost the margin she achieved on her sales. However, fitting in buying ingredients, baking and selling around schoolwork was tough, and she went back to selling second-hand goods online. She was doing fine with that, but then got into resale by chance, when she bought herself a hoodie on special offer. It was too small, but instead of sending it back, she resold it for double what she'd bought it for. Before long, the new business took off, and she spent everything she earned on more stock to sell.

It may seem as if Jade's success has come without much effort, but the contrary is true. She has to put hours of work into researching on social media which products are 'hot', so she knows what's currently popular enough to resell for significantly more than their original retail price. Jade also gets tips from other resellers on messaging platforms that she's joined. Even so, not all her choices turn out to be good ones, and some products 'brick', selling for less than she's paid for them. Luckily, others go for up to 400% more!

So what about the ethics of Jade's business practices? One criticism often levelled at the resell industry is that it pushes up the price of the things people most want, making them unaffordable for many. While Jade understands why no one's going to be happy about paying premium prices, she says, 'All I do is take advantage of rises in demand for certain products, especially when supply is limited, just like all entrepreneurs do!' But she adds that she only sells luxury brands in this way, never anything that is essential to people's health or well-being.

1 What is the writer doing in the first paragraph?
  A explaining recent changes in how people buy things
  B identifying the most effective internet-selling method
  C outlining ways of using the internet for financial gain
  D suggesting solutions to problems with online shopping

2 In the second paragraph, what do we learn about Jade's business?
  A Its fast growth has created a storage problem.
  B Its profits are expected to rise.
  C Its products vary across marketplaces.
  D Its costs are relatively low.

3 What does the writer say about how Jade started reselling?
  A She hadn't planned to take her business activities in that direction.
  B She did it in response to failing in one business venture.
  C She hadn't shown a talent for selling until recently.
  D She didn't make a large profit at first.

4 In the third paragraph, what does **margin** mean?
  A the level of Jade's losses
  B the amount that Jade increased her sales
  C the difference in profit between the different types of product Jade sold
  D the amount of money Jade made

5 What point is the writer making in the fourth paragraph?
  A Jade has managed to succeed surprisingly fast.
  B Jade is operating in a highly competitive market.
  C Jade's ability to recover from losses is remarkable.
  D Jade's line of business involves some challenges.

6 What is Jade's attitude towards her business practices?
  A She sees no reason for people to be critical of them.
  B She believes they are standard trading techniques.
  C She would like to change certain aspects of them.
  D She thinks it's important to try to ensure they are fair.

Speaking

A

B

Part 1
Page 108

1 🔊 17 Listen to two students answering some Speaking Part 1 questions and write down what they like and dislike.

	Like	Dislike
Lara		
Jacob		

2 🔊 17 Listen again and complete the phrases they use.

Like	Dislike	Neither like nor dislike
1 I'm .... art.	7 I'm .... playing rugby myself.	11 Well, history is OK but it's ....
2 I .... going to art galleries.	8 I .... playing other sports very much.	
3 I'm .... rugby, of course.		
4 I .... going to see them.	9 I'm .... going to the mountains in the summer.	
5 I'm .... skiing.		12 I .... doing science.
6 English and geography are	10 I .... going for long walks.	

✓ Exam task

Work in pairs to ask and answer the questions below. If your partner doesn't have much to say, use the questions in brackets to help.

💡 Exam tip

The examiner will ask you some questions about your everyday life, your free time and your school. This will include some questions about what you like.

- Do you prefer watching sports to playing them? (Why?)
- Do you enjoy watching TV? (Tell me about a programme you have watched recently.)
- Do you enjoy reading books? (What kind of books do you like? / Why don't you enjoy reading books?)
- What do you like doing on holiday? (Why do you enjoy it?)

Speaking

C

D

Part 2
💬 ›› Page 110

3 The photos on pages 56 and 57 show four different ways of shopping. Which of the ways do you prefer?

4 🔊 18 Listen to Adam, a student, talking in a Speaking exam. Which of the photos has Adam been given? Tick (✓) the ideas below which he mentions.

Advantages

> compare prices   convenient   for sale   latest fashions
> lots of choice   more fun   more unusual stuff
> other facilities   you can try clothes on

Disadvantages

> bad quality   can't try things on
> not much for teenagers   quite traditional
> too crowded   wait for the post

5 Complete the expressions Adam used when he didn't know what to say.

1 Mmm, ... me ....
2 .... me .... for a
   ....
3 Not .... would .... but
   I think …

6 Work in pairs. Write down other things you could say about the photographs Adam talked about.

7 Now look at the other two photographs. Can you use the same ideas to talk about these photos? Try to think of some more ideas and write them down.

✓ Exam task

Work in pairs. Choose two photographs each and compare them. What might people enjoy about shopping in these different ways? Time yourselves and talk for one minute each.

Here are some words you can use to connect your ideas about the photos.

> in both photos   on the other hand
> the difference is that   whereas

💡 Exam tips

- When you need to think, say something in English to give yourself time.
- While your partner is talking, think about your own opinion on the topic as the examiner will ask you a question at the end. You only need to say a sentence or two.

UNIT 7   57

Grammar

Verbs and expressions followed by *to* + infinitive or *-ing* form
>> Page 91

1. In Speaking Part 1 Lara and Jacob used these verbs and expressions. Which ones are followed by a *to* + infinitive and which by the *-ing* form of the verb? Put them by the correct heading.

   attempt   can't bear   don't mind   enjoy   hope   be interested in   be keen on   like   love   prefer   want   would like   would prefer

   to + infinitive: ………………………………………………………
   -ing form: ………………………………………………………
   either *to* + infinitive or *-ing* form: ………………………………

2. Exam candidates often make mistakes with verb forms. Choose the correct form in these sentences and add any new verbs to the headings in Exercise 1.
   1. If you are **going / to go** to the beach, just take some cold drinks with you because it'll be very hot.
   2. We'll **meeting / meet** you outside the hospital.
   3. I want **come / to come** back next week.
   4. I suggested **walking / to walk** along the beach last night.
   5. I want **going / to go** to the cinema to watch a film.
   6. Parents never want you **go / to go** somewhere dangerous.
   7. I've always dreamed of **to live / living** in the big city.
   8. I would like **visit / to visit** you in the summer.
   9. I prefer **to buy / buy** clothes with my own money.
   10. I enjoy **playing / play** tennis because it's my favourite sport.

Reported speech
>> Page 92

3. Complete the reported speech with the verbs in the correct tense and any other words necessary.
   1. 'I work in the marketing department.'
      He said he …………………… in the marketing department.
   2. 'I'm having a late lunch.'
      She phoned to say that she …………………… a late lunch.
   3. 'I've never ridden a motorbike.'
      He told me that he …………………… a motorbike.
   4. 'I got food poisoning from the meat I ate.'
      She suggested that she …………………… food poisoning from the meat that she …………………… .
   5. 'I'll ring as soon as I get home.'
      He promised that he …………………… as soon as he …………………… home.
   6. 'I can play the guitar, but I can't play the piano.'
      She told me that she …………………… play the guitar but that she …………………… play the piano.

4. Look at these two questions. Write the reported sentences. When do we use *if* in the reported sentence?

   How are you?   The girl's mum asked her …………………… .

   Do you want to come shopping?   The girl's mum asked …………………… .

5. Now report these questions.
   1. 'Why are you so sad?'
      The woman asked her son …………………… .
   2. 'What are you listening to?'
      The girl's father asked her …………………… .
   3. 'Did your team win?'
      The girl asked the boy …………………… .
   4. 'Are there any leftovers?'
      The girl asked her mother …………………… .
   5. 'Have you seen my wallet?'
      The man asked his wife …………………… .
   6. 'Will you be home late?'
      The boy's mother asked him …………………… .

Reading and Use of English

6 Which of these verbs fit into the gap in the sentence below? Which ones don't fit? Why?

> advised   agreed   asked   encouraged
> explained   mentioned   persuaded
> reminded   said   told   warned

The girl's mum .... her to clean the kitchen.

7 Choose the correct verb in these sentences.
1. The teacher **told** / **explained** the children to bring some extra money for the trip.
2. We had **agreed** / **advised** to meet on Thursday morning.
3. The weather forecaster **encouraged** / **warned** that there might be some showers.
4. I forgot to **mention** / **remind** that we've got a bit more time.

8 Exam candidates often make mistakes with reported speech. Choose the correct verb in these sentences.
1. They **spoke** / **said** that the weather would be nice, but it rained all weekend.
2. Pamela **told** / **said** her brother to wait for her outside.
3. In your text you **told** / **asked** me if there was anything to do in Scotland.
4. I **told them** / **told** my name and date of birth.
5. Harry accidentally **told to** / **told** his sister Lisa that her friends had arranged a surprise party for her birthday.
6. I **asked** / **said** my mother to drive me to the shops.
7. Annie **told** / **asked** her sister that she could open her present now.
8. I **said to** / **asked** my parents for permission to go, but it was obvious that they didn't want me to.

Part 4

1 Match the phrases that mean the same.

1	less happy than	a	I borrowed
2	warned me not to	b	was once happy
3	wasn't taught	c	such a happy
4	lent me	d	happier than
5	so happy	e	said I shouldn't
6	stop	f	wish I had done
7	used to be happy	g	more unhappy than
8	I regret not doing	h	instead of
9	not as unhappy as	i	give up
10	rather than	j	didn't learn

Exam task

For questions **1–6**, complete the second sentence so that it has a similar meaning to the first sentence, using the word given. **Do not change the word given**. You must use between **two** and **five** words, including the word given.

Example

0 The film went on so long that they missed the bus home.
SUCH
It was .... *such a long film* .... that they missed the bus home.

1 Dad said I shouldn't cycle to school because a storm was forecast.
WARNED
Dad .... cycle to school because a storm was forecast.

2 No other school in the region has more successful students than ours.
THE
Our school has .... students in the region.

3 The children regretted going to the museum and not the theme park.
WISHED
The children .... to the theme park, not the museum.

4 Nisha had a healthy salad instead of choosing her usual burger and fries.
GOING
Nisha had a healthy salad rather .... her usual burger and fries.

5 'Did you see Uncle Fred at Grandma's?' Dad asked me.
SEEN
Dad asked me .... Uncle Fred at Grandma's.

6 The teacher said to Ben, 'Don't forget your waterproof coat tomorrow for the forest walk.'
REMINDED
The teacher .... bring his waterproof coat the next day for the forest walk.

Exam tip

In Reading and Use of English Part 4, always try to write something because each question is worth two marks.

UNIT 7

Listening

PEOPLE AND FEELINGS

1. Look at photos A, B and C. Work in pairs and discuss these questions.
   1. Which of the words below best describes the feeling in each photo?
   2. Why do you think they might be feeling like this?

   > amused   anxious   astonished
   > calm   concerned   confused
   > curious   furious   irritated

2. Look at all the feelings in Exercise 1. In pairs, tell each other about a time when you felt one of these emotions.

3. Match what someone has said with how they are feeling.

   1. Come and watch this video with me – it's hilarious!
   2. I wonder how animals can live in hot, dry deserts. Do you know?
   3. I've had a long, hot bath and it's taken away all my stress.
   4. Oh no! There's rice everywhere! I wish they'd make these rice packets easier to get into!

   a calm   b irritated   c amused   d curious

4. 🔊 19 Listen to a young man describing his best friends. What kind of person is each friend? Choose A, B or C.

   Friend 1 is …
   A usually calm   B usually anxious   C usually curious

   Friend 2 is …
   A often confused about issues
   B often amused about issues
   C often concerned about issues

   Friend 3 is …
   A rarely anxious   B rarely furious   C rarely amused

Part 3

✓ Exam task

🔊 20 You will hear five short extracts in which teenagers are talking about how an influencer on social media made them feel.

For questions **1–5**, choose from the list (**A–H**) how each speaker felt. Use the letters only once. There are three extra letters which you do not need to use.

> **💡 Exam tip**
> Before listening, think about what words or expressions might be used to indicate the meaning of each answer option.

A I became obsessed with their ideas.
B I was astonished at what they could do.
C I was inspired to change some habits.
D I became calmer.
E I got irritated by their approach.
F I got anxious about what they said.
G I was eager to share their ideas with others.
H I was amused by some of their posts.

Speaker 1 — 1
Speaker 2 — 2
Speaker 3 — 3
Speaker 4 — 4
Speaker 5 — 5

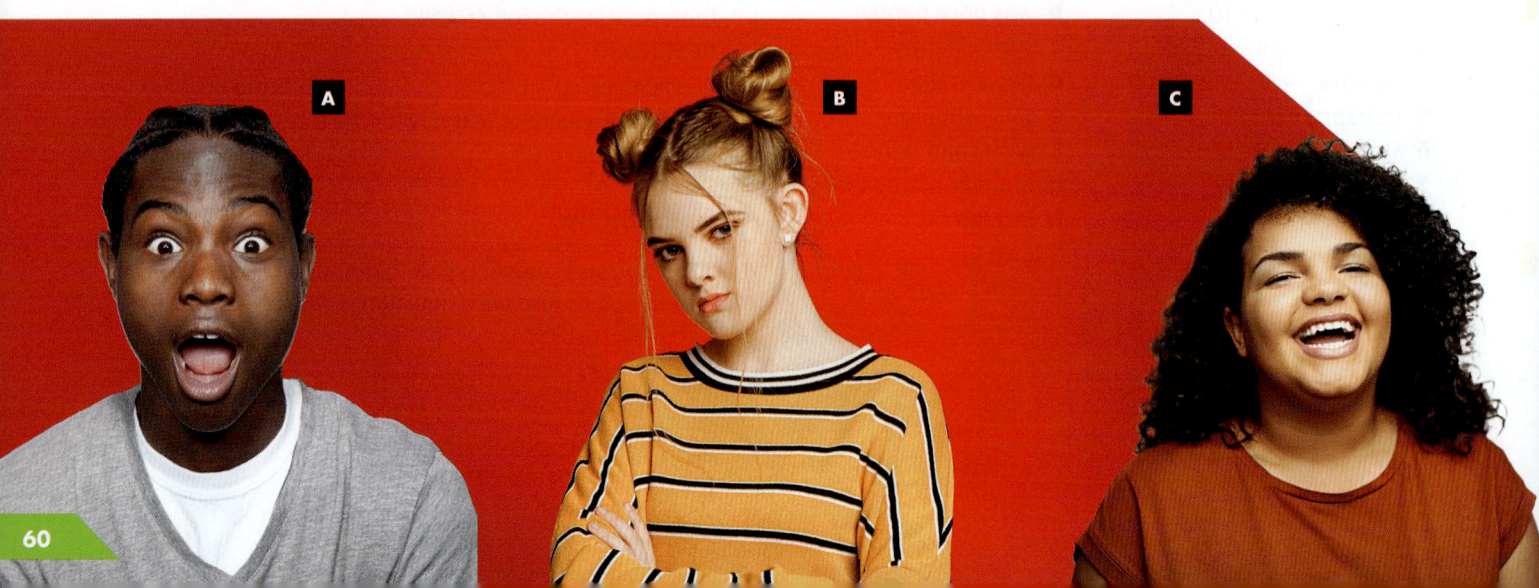

60

Writing

Part 2 email / letter

>> Page 98

1 Read this exam task and the letter from Emma on the right. Work in pairs to complete the letter with the words and phrases from the box below, with capital letters where necessary.

You have received this letter from your English friend Lauren.

> ... and I'm doing a project at school. We have to find which famous people teenagers admire, and why. Can you choose a famous person you admire and write and tell me why you admire them? It'll be interesting to see who you've chosen!
>
> Thanks for helping me, Lauren

Write your **letter**.

| another reason   apart from the fact that |
| even   managed to   not because |
| one of the main ones   that said   yet |

2 Highlight the adjectives Emma used to describe Sheku Kanneh Mason's personality in the letter.

3 Which famous person would you write about? Work in pairs and do the following.

1 Tell your partner who you have chosen and why he or she is or was famous.
2 Tick (✓) any of the adjectives in the letter you can use to describe him or her.
3 Make a note of any other adjectives you want to use.

4 Write your own answer to Lauren.

Remember to:
- begin and end your letter correctly.
- start by saying who you admire and why.
- explain why the person is or was famous.
- use some of the linking words and adjectives in Exercises 1 and 2.

5 Is there a person in your family, or a student in your school/college that you admire? Work in pairs and do the following.

1 Tell your partner who you have chosen and why.
2 Write down any adjectives you can use to describe him/her.
3 Do the exam task on the right.

Dear Lauren

You asked me to tell you about a famous person I admire. One of the people I admire most is a musician called Sheku Kanneh Mason. (1) .... he's an extremely talented cello player, there are plenty more reasons to admire him. (2) .... for me is the fact that he's black, like me, and has (3) .... succeed in an industry where that's unusual. (4) .... I admire him is the fact that he plays classical music – not what most young people consider cool, but that doesn't bother him. He's a strong, determined, genuine person, doing something because he's passionate about it, (5) .... his mates are doing it or because it's trendy. (6) .... , he does enjoy more normal teenage things too, like playing football.

I've watched interviews with him, and he actually seems quite a shy person. (7) .... he's played in some of the largest, most famous concert halls in the world, released a chart-topping album and won many awards. He's (8) .... played at a British royal wedding!

I'm sure you can see why I think he's so amazing!
Best wishes
Emma

✓ Exam task

Write an answer to this exam task. Write **140–190** words in an appropriate style.

You have received this email from your Australian friend, Andrew.

I'm doing a project at school. We have to find out which person in their family teenagers admire, and why. Can you choose one person in your family who you admire and write and tell me why? Thanks for helping me.

Andrew

Write your **email**.

UNIT 7   61

8 Breakthrough

TECHNOLOGY

A

B

Reading and Use of English

1 Look at the photos. Which picture does each of these terms describe?

> early mobile phone   dial-up telephone
> smartphone   smartwatch

2 Work in pairs. Discuss what features each type of phone had/has. Use these words.

> apps   battery   black and white screen
> camera   charger   colour screen
> dial   external antenna   GPS
> internet   landline connection
> light weight   heavy weight   mobile network
> push buttons   text messaging   touchscreen
> wearable device   wi-fi

3 How do you do the following on your phone?

use an internet browser   bookmark a webpage
protect against viruses   send attachments
charge the battery   update software
back data up

4 How do you think telecommunications will change in the future?

5 Look at the list of inventions. Discuss which is the most useful invention and why.

air conditioning   freezer
television   sewing machine
fridge   camera
washing machine   microwave oven

Part 7

✓ **Exam task**

You are going to read an article about four young inventors. For questions **1–10**, choose from the people (**A–D**). The people may be chosen more than once.

Which person

invents things using an aspect of technology they have a fascination for?	1
decided to create a device after a surprising discovery?	2
developed concern about an issue while pursuing hobbies?	3
invented a device that warns of environmental factors that can worsen some medical conditions?	4
was known as someone full of curiosity?	5
designed a device that restricted access to a place?	6
designed some technology that works using renewable energy?	7
gained the inspiration for a solution from a chance discovery?	8
has an ambition to have a widespread impact on people?	9
focused on creating a device that would help local people?	10

💡 **Exam tip**

Make sure the meaning of the question really matches the text you choose as your answer: topics or ideas in the questions are usually mentioned in more than one text.

Reading and Use of English

Young inventors

A Riya Karumanchi

Riya was 14 when she saw her friend's grandma, who had poor eyesight, using a white stick to find her way around her home. Riya, living up to her childhood nickname 'the question box', asked how it worked and was astonished to learn it was in fact just a stick, not the high-tech gadget she'd assumed. Furthermore, it had been around for 100 years without being updated. So she designed the 'SmartCane', a device which uses sensors to identify a wide variety of obstacles and dangers such as wet surfaces, and then vibrates to alert the user. It also has a navigation system which can find safe routes. Riya's ultimate dream is to become what she calls a 'unicorn person'. Instead of creating a 'unicorn company' with a valuation of a billion dollars, she wants to make a positive difference to a billion individuals.

B Neil Deshmukh

Younger siblings using your things can be very annoying. 14-year-old Neil had a younger brother who was constantly in his room, using his computer games. Neil got so fed up that he invented a device to keep his brother out of his bedroom. The device used AI – artificial intelligence – to recognise different faces, and would only unlock the bedroom door for Neil. Since then, Neil's created a range of apps and devices using AI, a field which he says he's 'super interested in'. One app uses crowdsourced data to help farmers around the globe identify and treat crop diseases, another provides spoken descriptions of photographs so that people with sight problems can 'see' them. One device he's invented indicates various levels of air quality by lighting up a fabric flower in different ways. This alerts people with asthma, lung disease or pollen allergies of the need to take steps to protect themselves.

C Xóchitl Guadalupe Cruz López

By the age of eight, Xóchitl had already won a national prize for extracting the aroma from flowers – an incredible achievement, but she didn't stop there! She made up her mind to do something about a problem affecting her own family as well as many of her neighbours. The only way they could heat water was to cut down trees and burn them, which was bad news for the environment. She also noticed the high rate of respiratory diseases in her neighbourhood, and thought this may be caused by the lack of access to water heaters: people often showered in cold water, despite the cold climate. Xóchitl came up with the idea of a solar-powered water heater made from recycled materials. Her invention is a very cheap device which can be installed on the roofs of houses, and consists of water bottles, a rubber hose, logs, black paint, and cheap plastic materials.

D Fionn Ferreira

When Fionn was growing up, he lived on the coast, where he went kayaking and swimming. These pastimes raised his awareness of the problem of marine plastic, especially microplastics – pieces less than five millimetres long. At the age of 12, he began looking for a way of removing microplastics from water. One day when walking along the shore, he found a lump of oil with plastic attached to it. There was nothing uncommon about this, but he suddenly realised that oil could be used to capture plastic from water. He made some 'ferrofluid', a magnetic liquid made from vegetable oil and iron oxide. When he poured it into water, microplastics from a wide range of rubbish, including plastic bottles and man-made fabrics, attached themselves to it. He then used a magnet to remove the ferrofluid and the attached microplastics, leaving behind only water. He'd like his invention to be used to remove microplastics from wastewater before it reaches the sea.

Grammar

Relative clauses
>> Page 93

1 Complete these sentences about the texts on page 63 with *who*, *which* or *where*.

Defining clauses
1 Her invention is a very cheap device .... can be installed on the roofs of houses.
2 Another app helps people .... are visually impaired to 'see'.
3 One device .... he's invented indicates various levels of air quality.
4 If you have a younger sibling .... is always using your things, you know how annoying it can be.
5 Neil's created a range of apps and devices using AI, a field .... he says he's 'super interested in'.

Non-defining clauses
6 He lived on the coast, ... he went kayaking and swimming.
7 Riya was 14 when she saw her friend's grandma, ... had poor eyesight, using a white stick.
8 The only way they could heat water was to cut down trees and burn them, ... was bad news for the environment.

2 Now answer these questions.
1 In which sentences could you leave out *who*, *which* or *where*? Why?
2 In which sentences could you put *that* instead of *who* or *which*?
3 What is the difference in punctuation between defining and non-defining clauses?

3 Read the question and the first two paragraphs of a candidate's essay. Complete the text with relative pronouns, indicating where *that* or no pronoun are possible alternatives.

> **All students should study science until they are at least 18. Do you agree?**
> Notes
> Write about:
> 1 which jobs need knowledge of science
> 2 whether all students are good at science
> 3 (your own idea)

> I certainly agree that all students should study science at school. It's a subject (1) .... is incredibly important in our world today. However, I think the issue of how long students should study is more difficult. If you are the kind of student (2) .... main interest is to become a doctor or a physicist, then certainly you will want to study science until you are 18. You will probably enjoy it too, because science is the subject (3) .... you are interested in, and probably the one (4) .... you are good at.
>
> But less able students, (5) .... find it difficult to pass exams in physics, biology and chemistry, will not be enthusiastic. These subjects, (6) .... can be hard at higher levels, may prove too challenging for them. The students will then get frustrated with science, (7) .... means they will behave badly in class. That will make things very difficult for the teachers (8) .... are responsible for them.

Writing

Part 1 essay
>> Page 96

1. Read the question and choose the correct adverbs in this essay. Use a dictionary if you need to.

Playing video games is a valuable way to spend your time. Do you agree?
Notes
Write about:
1 the benefits of playing video games
2 not being active
3 (your own idea)

Many people of all ages spend a great deal of time gaming, **(1) primarily / totally** because it's so enjoyable. When you play video games, you escape into another world and feel like you're a different person. This can be **(2) really / slightly** valuable if you have problems in your life, or even if you're **(3) still / just** feeling bored. As well as these benefits, gaming can improve some physical skills, such as your hand-eye coordination and your speed of reaction. Games that involve strategies also improve your thinking skills. Playing games with friends can **(4) well / even** develop some social skills.

However, one major problem with spending time gaming is that you **(5) normally / completely** sit down to do it. Therefore, if you spend several hours gaming, you are inactive for a long time. In addition, video games are played inside, so you don't get any fresh air. These aspects of gaming can **(6) undoubtedly / uncertainly** have a very negative impact on your health.

To conclude, I would say that playing video games can **(7) firmly / definitely** be valuable in some ways, but only if a limited amount of time is spent doing it each week. This ensures you have time for more active outdoor activities, too.

2. Work in pairs. Discuss these questions.
1 How many paragraphs are there?
2 What is the writer's 'own idea' in the essay?
3 Do you think the essay is an effective answer to the question?

3. It's useful to use topic-specific vocabulary in your essay. Make a list of any vocabulary or phrases about gaming in the essay that you could use in one of your own.

 **Exam task**

 **Exam tip**

You can improve the mark for your essay by using a range of vocabulary to express your ideas.

Write an answer to the essay question below. Write your answer in **140–190** words in an appropriate style, for homework.

In your English class you have been talking about great inventions. Now your English teacher has asked you to write an essay for homework.
Write your essay using **all** the notes and giving reasons for your point of view.
Do you think that the aeroplane is the greatest invention of all time?
Notes
Write about:
1 the advantages of flying
2 the impact on natural environments
3 (your own idea)

Remember to:
• plan your essay carefully so that your argument is logical.
• make sure you answer the question, use both the prompts, add an idea of your own and come to a clear conclusion.
• use a range of vocabulary, including a variety of adverbs, to make your meaning clearer and more precise.

UNIT 8   65

Reading and Use of English

Vocabulary – Science

1 What do these icons represent? Write these scientific subjects under the most appropriate pictures.

> astronomy   chemistry   ecology   electronics
> engineering   medicine   psychology
> telecommunications

2 Read the topics in the left-hand column. Write one scientific subject from Exercise 1 that each set is generally studied in.

Topics	Scientific subject
endangered species, conservation, pollution, ecosystems	
AI, robotics, computer chips	
acids, gases, metals, atoms, chemical substances	
cells, human biology, diseases, genetics	

3 Complete these sentences with one word from Exercise 2.

1. Aluminium is a useful .... because it is so light.
2. Oxygen is a .... in the Earth's atmosphere that we can breathe.
3. Carbon dioxide has one carbon ....
4. Rice is a .... of grass.
5. Human health is determined by .... as well as lifestyle.
6. Microplastic in oceans damages their fragile ....

Vocabulary – Word building (3)

4 Write the nouns, adjectives and adverbs of these nouns.

Nouns ending *logy* (subjects of study)	Nouns referring to a person (*y* + *ist*)	Adjective (*y* + *ical*)	Adverb (*y* + *ically*)
biology	biologist	biological	biologically
psychology			
ecology			
technology			
geology			

5 Which of these suffixes can be added to make nouns and which to make adjectives?

> -al   -er   -ful   -ible   -ic   -ity   -ive
> -ment   -ness   -ship   -sion   -tion

To make nouns, add: ....
To make adjectives, add: ....

6 Read the text below. Which gaps must be completed with nouns and which with adjectives?

Nouns: ....
Adjectives: ....

What do ecologists do?

Ecologists study the **(1)** .... between plants, animals and the environment they inhabit. They tend to work for governments and other organisations such as charities that carry out **(2)** .... research and habitat conservation. A **(3)** .... part of their work is to report on the **(4)** .... of damage being caused to an ecosystem by proposed construction work.

Ecologists spend part of their time conducting **(5)** .... that involve classifying plants, animals and other organisms, and recording data. They spend the rest of their time in the laboratory or office, carrying out analysis and **(6)** .... of this data.

They then have to present the data in a clear and **(7)** .... way to government officials, engineers, architects, town **(8)** .... and members of the public.

Reading and Use of English

7 Now use some of the noun and adjective suffixes in Exercise 5 on page 66, and these words to complete the text in Exercise 6.

1 relate
2 environment
3 centre
4 probable
5 investigate
6 evaluate
7 access
8 plan

8 Choose the correct ending to the statement.

If you add the prefix *dis-*, *im-*, *il-*, *in-*, *ir-*, *mis-* or *un-* to the beginning of a word (for example *possible – impossible*), it gives the word

A a stronger meaning.
B the opposite meaning.
C a similar meaning.

9 Write the words next to the prefix that can be used with them.

approval   believable   experienced
fortunately   honesty   legally   patiently
polite   regular   reliable   responsible
satisfied   understanding

dis-	
im-	
il-	
in-	
mis-	
un-	
ir-	

Part 3

💡 Exam tips

- Some gaps in Part 3 must be filled with a word formed with a prefix. Sometimes it will need a suffix as well.
- When you are completing a gap with a noun, think about whether it needs to be singular or plural.
- Read the text through before you begin, and read it again when you have finished, to be sure it makes sense with the new words you have written.

✓ Exam task

For questions **1–8**, read the text below. Use the word given in capitals at the end of some of the lines to form a word that fits in the gap **in the same line**. There is an example at the beginning (**0**).

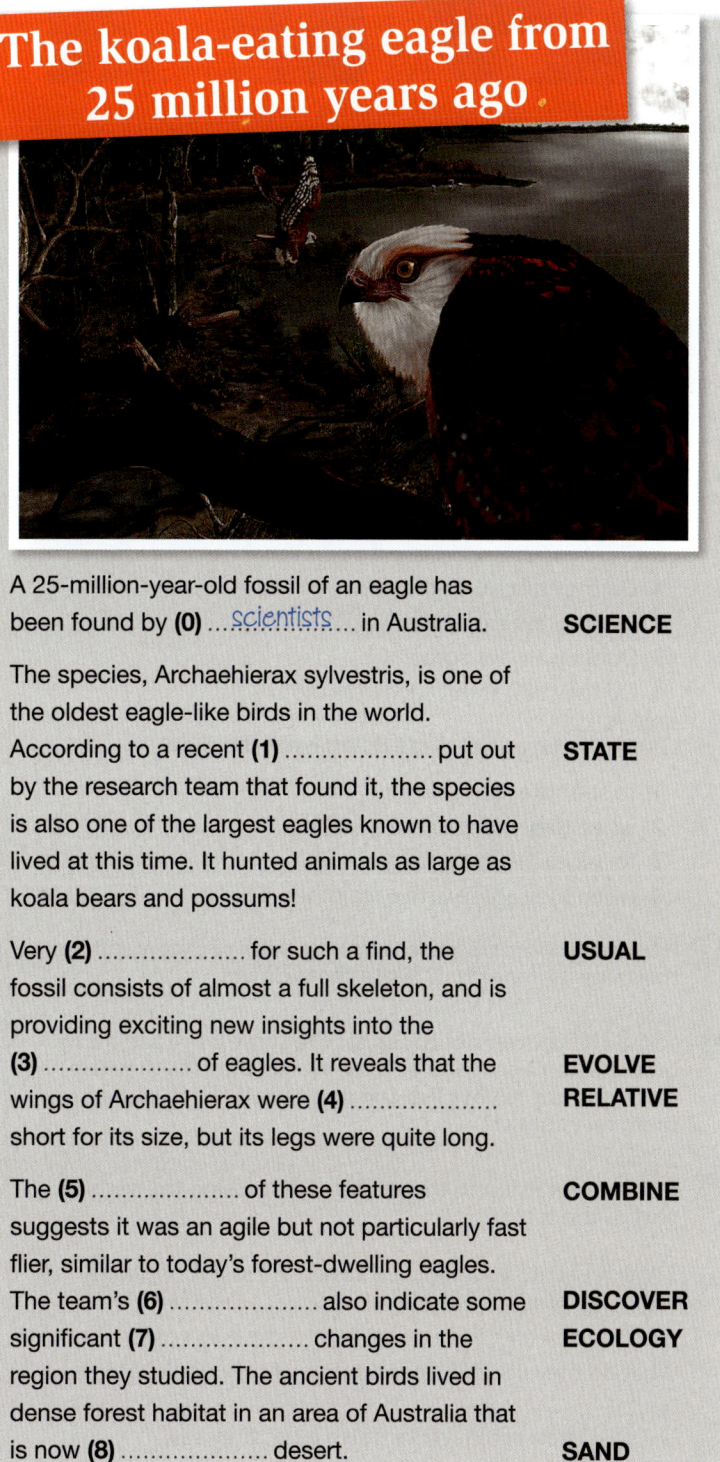

The koala-eating eagle from 25 million years ago

A 25-million-year-old fossil of an eagle has been found by (**0**) ...*scientists*... in Australia.   **SCIENCE**

The species, Archaehierax sylvestris, is one of the oldest eagle-like birds in the world. According to a recent (**1**) .... put out   **STATE**
by the research team that found it, the species is also one of the largest eagles known to have lived at this time. It hunted animals as large as koala bears and possums!

Very (**2**) .... for such a find, the   **USUAL**
fossil consists of almost a full skeleton, and is providing exciting new insights into the
(**3**) .... of eagles. It reveals that the   **EVOLVE**
wings of Archaehierax were (**4**) ....   **RELATIVE**
short for its size, but its legs were quite long.

The (**5**) .... of these features   **COMBINE**
suggests it was an agile but not particularly fast flier, similar to today's forest-dwelling eagles.
The team's (**6**) .... also indicate some   **DISCOVER**
significant (**7**) .... changes in the   **ECOLOGY**
region they studied. The ancient birds lived in dense forest habitat in an area of Australia that is now (**8**) .... desert.   **SAND**

UNIT 8   67

Speaking

Part 3
>> Page 114

1 Work in pairs. Talk about your mobile phone. Give reasons for your answers.

How often do you use it?
How important is it to you?

2 🔊 21 Listen to two students discussing this question.

> How important are these inventions in our daily lives?
> fridge   TV   car   bicycle   laptop

1 Do they take turns to talk?
2 Do they ask each other's opinions?
3 Do they always agree?
4 Do they talk about each invention?

3 🔊 21 Listen again. Write down what they say.

1 to start the conversation.
2 when they move to the next item.
3 to ask each other's opinions.
4 when they agree with each other.

4 How many words/phrases can you think of that mean the same as *important*? Write them down.

5 🔊 21 It is better not to repeat the same word too many times. Listen again and add the words/phrases they use for *important* to your list. Did you already have some of them on your list?

6 🔊 22 Now listen to the students discussing the second part of the test.

> Which two do you think will become less important in the future?

What do they decide? Does it matter if they don't agree?

7 🔊 22 Listen again. Write down what they say.

1 How does Karolina begin?
2 What does Miguel say when he asks Karolina's opinion?
3 What does Miguel say about the bicycle to show he hasn't changed his mind?

✓ Exam task

Work in pairs. Time your discussion. If it is too short, think of other things you can say.

Here are some inventions that many people think are important in our daily lives.

Talk to each other about how important these things are in our daily lives.

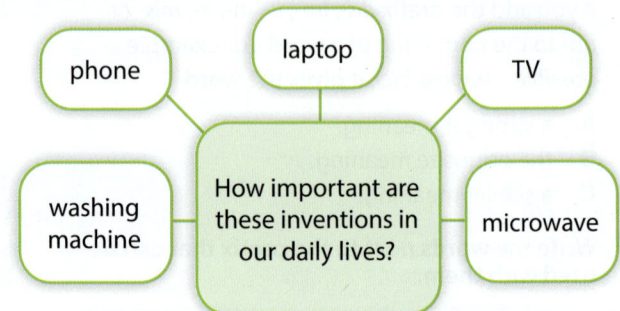

Now you have about a minute to decide which two you think will become more important in the future.

💡 Exam tip

Don't spend too long discussing one item. You only have three minutes for the whole conversation. Learn phrases you can use to move the conversation forwards. See Units 4 and 6.

Part 4
>> Page 116

✓ Exam task

Discuss these questions with a partner.

- How important is technology at school? Which subjects is it essential for? Why?
- Do you enjoy watching TV? What programmes do you like? Why?
- Do you think the use of technology has stopped people from talking to each other? Why? / Why not?
- Do you think people are too dependent on mobile phones? Why? / Why not?
- Some people say young children shouldn't watch TV. Do you agree? Why? / Why not?

💡 Exam tip

When you answer a question, think about why, when or how. Always extend your answer.

Listening

Part 1

1 Work in pairs. Quickly read the eight questions below and match the situations with A–H.

A exchanging opinions
B describing the differences between things
C identifying a choice someone makes
D giving an opinion
E identifying the type of something
F giving the main idea about something
G expressing feelings about something
H identifying the origin of something

> **Exam tip**
>
> When you read the question and possible answers before listening, imagine the situation and what the person or two people might say.

Exam task

🔊 **23** You will hear people talking in eight different situations. For questions **1–8**, choose the best answer, **A**, **B** or **C**.

1 You hear a boy who lived in Spain telling a friend in England about his New Year's Eve.
   What does he say about eating grapes on New Year's Eve?
   A It makes people feel closer to each other.
   B It's impossible for anyone to do quickly enough.
   C It encourages people to have fun.

2 You hear a boy telling his friend about going on a ghost walk in London.
   How did the boy feel about the walk?
   A He was disappointed after going on it.
   B He was reluctant to go on it.
   C He was afraid to go on it.

3 You hear a girl talking to her father about music lessons.
   What instrument is the girl going to have lessons in?
   A the cello
   B the trumpet
   C the bass guitar

4 You hear two friends talking about a school football match. The girl and the boy agree that
   A the girl's sister scored the best goal.
   B the opponents nearly won the match.
   C their team's goalie played very well.

5 You hear a boy talking about the geography course he's doing.
   What is the boy doing?
   A comparing the course to other similar courses
   B explaining how difficult it was to choose a course
   C complaining about certain aspects of the course

6 You hear the introduction to a podcast about waste plastic. The woman says the podcast aims to
   A tell listeners about some solutions to the issue of plastic waste.
   B encourage listeners to recycle more of the plastic they use.
   C warn listeners of the damage being caused by plastic pollution.

7 You hear a boy talking to his mother about a jacket he's just got.
   Where did the boy get the jacket from?
   A an online store
   B a friend
   C a charity shop

8 You hear a report on a science event.
   What kind of event is described in the report?
   A a research project
   B a competition
   C a workshop

UNIT 8

Revision

UNIT 1

1 Correct the mistakes in these sentences.

1 I'm very sorry, but I'm not understanding the instructions.
2 I'm excited for our summer trip. We camp in a forest.
3 John thinks that woman over there is famous, but I don't recognising her.
4 This time tomorrow we'll sit on a plane to the USA.
5 Do I need to text you when I'll arrive?
6 I'll have to call you back – I can't talk right now because I clean my room.
7 Let me know once you'll hear from Joanna.
8 Children who are coming from large families find it easier to share things.

2 Complete the second sentence so that it has a similar meaning to the first sentence, using the word given. Do not change the word given. You must use between two and five words, including the word given.

1 Usually, a modern city has wider streets than a historic city.
AS
Usually, the streets in a historic city
.... those in a modern city.

2 Industrial areas tend to be very noisy compared to rural areas.
FAR
There is usually
.... in industrial areas than in rural areas.

3 It takes my brother two hours to get to work but our father has a two-minute walk.
MUCH
My brother's journey to work
.... our father's.

4 My favourite café is near the market square.
BEST
The café which I
.... from the market square.

5 My friends and I don't go to the cinema as often as our parents do.
LESS
My friends and I go to the cinema
.... our parents do.

3 Decide which answer (A, B, C or D) best fits each gap.

1 There was a .... of opinion in my family about what we should have for dinner, so in the end we all made our own.
  A variation B contrast C difference D disagreement
2 We found a quiet .... to sit down and read our books.
  A point B spot C situation D site
3 If you want to be a professional athlete, you will need to .... an effort to practise.
  A do B give C make D take
4 If you go on a seaside holiday, you will get lots of .... air.
  A fresh B pure C clean D natural
5 Brian speaks loudly to .... attention to himself.
  A pull B draw C focus D catch
6 My dad will make a .... decision tonight about whether I can attend the party.
  A last B latest C finishing D final
7 When Eddie found out everyone knew his secret, he realised he was in serious ....
  A trouble B problem C fault D concern
8 I find .... my breath for a long time difficult, so I'm not very good at swimming under water.
  A keeping B cutting C stopping D holding

4 Read this email and choose the correct form of the verbs.

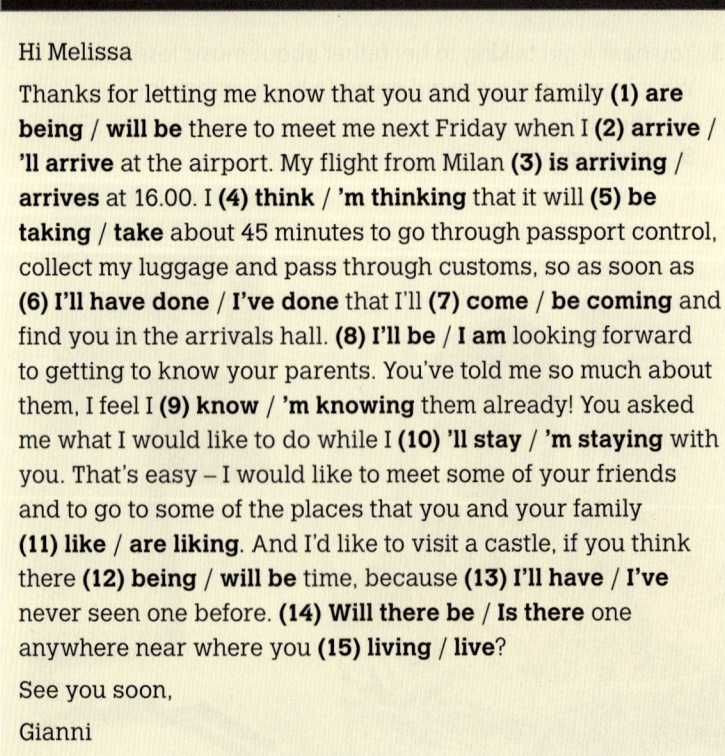

Hi Melissa

Thanks for letting me know that you and your family **(1) are being / will be** there to meet me next Friday when I **(2) arrive / 'll arrive** at the airport. My flight from Milan **(3) is arriving / arrives** at 16.00. I **(4) think / 'm thinking** that it will **(5) be taking / take** about 45 minutes to go through passport control, collect my luggage and pass through customs, so as soon as **(6) I'll have done / I've done** that I'll **(7) come / be coming** and find you in the arrivals hall. **(8) I'll be / I am** looking forward to getting to know your parents. You've told me so much about them, I feel I **(9) know / 'm knowing** them already! You asked me what I would like to do while I **(10) 'll stay / 'm staying** with you. That's easy – I would like to meet some of your friends and to go to some of the places that you and your family **(11) like / are liking**. And I'd like to visit a castle, if you think there **(12) being / will be** time, because **(13) I'll have / I've** never seen one before. **(14) Will there be / Is there** one anywhere near where you **(15) living / live**?

See you soon,
Gianni

 Now go to Practice Extra Unit 1

Revision

UNIT 2

1 Match the two halves of the sentences and put the verbs into the correct past tense.

1 I hurt my knee
2 They got to the restaurant so late that
3 We haven't spoken
4 I've been trying to finish my homework all morning
5 I called you six times yesterday
6 We've been to the new shopping centre several times
7 I was already cycling to the café
8 He doesn't know his way around the town

a but you .... (not answer).
b but I .... (not manage) to do it yet.
c when you .... (send) me the message to cancel.
d while I .... (run) to catch the bus.
e because he .... (not be) there before.
f the kitchen .... (already close).
g but we .... (not buy) anything from there yet.
h since we .... (have) an argument.

2 Complete the text with the verbs from the box, in the correct tense.

| be x2 | go | have | invite | know |
| let | set | shine | skateboard | |

My sister (1) .... skateboarding every weekend with her friends. She always says, 'When you (2) .... a bit older you can come with me.' I (3) .... 15 next winter, so maybe she (4) .... me go with her then. My brother also loves skateboarding and he has a really cool skateboard. Last weekend he (5) .... me to go out with him. I (6) .... (never) with him before so I was really pleased. When we (7) .... out, the sun (8) ...., but after about half an hour it started to rain. I (9) .... skateboarding lessons since March, so I (10) .... that I could cope. My uncle was really surprised when we got back and my brother told him how good I am at skateboarding!

3 Complete the sentences with adverbs formed from the adjectives from the box. Use each adjective only once.

| careful | definite | easy | excited | immediate |
| particular | simple | usual | | |

1 The children shouted .... when the show began.
2 José says he'll .... come to the game tomorrow. He can't wait.
3 Tom is a really quick learner – he can memorise things ....
4 Football practice is starting in five minutes so we need to get changed ....
5 I .... go to bed early, but sometimes I won't sleep until late.
6 My dad put the TV down very .... as he didn't want to break it!
7 I explained the situation as .... as I could but they still didn't understand it.
8 Ellie was .... good at long-distance running so her parents helped her to sign up for a marathon.

4 Complete the sentences with an adjective formed from one of the words from the box.

| adventure | centre | fury | mystery | nature | predict | rely | suit |

1 I opened the letter but there was nothing inside the envelope – it was very ....
2 It's .... to feel anxious when you are away from home.
3 My parents like to go to a different place each holiday – they're quite ....
4 My cousin is looking for someone .... to look after her house while she is away.
5 This film isn't .... for my siblings as they're very young.
6 My brother was .... when he found out that I had eaten his sweets.
7 My parents always make the same jokes to each other – they're so ....
8 My house is very ....; there are lots of shops nearby.

 Now go to Practice Extra Unit 2

Revision

UNIT 3

1 Circle the correct linking words. Sometimes both are correct.
1 **While / Although** she could sing very well, Tanya could not play any musical instruments.
2 **Despite / Even though** he loved sailing, he couldn't swim!
3 **Despite / Although** I like going to school, I much prefer the weekends.
4 **In spite of / Although** Nick tried hard to be on time, he was almost always late.
5 **In spite of / Despite** not being a fan of superhero films, Georgia really enjoyed the latest Marvel TV series.
6 **In spite of / Even though** he is good with computers, Cameron simply isn't interested in them.
7 **While / Despite** enjoying art, I wouldn't want to study it at college.
8 **Although / Despite** I dislike cats, they've never scared me.

2 Complete the sentences with the passive form of the verb.
1 Our grammar test .... (cancel) because a lot of students still needed practice.
2 I .... (send) to a summer camp this year because it will build up my self-confidence.
3 I .... (tell) not to do anything too dangerous for my science project.
4 The party .... (organise) by my closest friend.
5 The package .... (deliver) next Wednesday.
6 I'm not buying a new graduation dress; it .... (make) by my mother.
7 I have to take the rugby trophy back to school, because it .... (display) on a special shelf this term.
8 Those books .... (return) to the school library.

3 Complete the sentences with the words from the box.

> camera operator   costume designer   director
> live performance   producer   scriptwriter
> set designer   sound technician

1 The .... usually checks the quality of the recording on a film.
2 The person who writes the play or film is called a ....
3 People often go to concerts and theatre productions because they enjoy ....
4 A .... is responsible for raising money to make a film.
5 A .... films the scenes and goes on location if necessary.
6 The .... guides and instructs the actors on how to perform a scene.
7 A .... creates the clothes the actors wear on set.
8 The .... arranges the scenery on the film set / theatre stage.

4 Which type of film would usually feature the following?
1 a spaceship, time travel and lots of special effects
2 funny scenes that make you laugh
3 a complicated plot with twists and turns
4 interesting factual information
5 cowboys and horses
6 characters that are drawn
7 moving figures or animals rather than real people
8 really frightening scenes, ghosts and monsters
9 car chases and people running across roofs
10 an amusing love story

5 Answer these questions about music.
1 Can you name two musical instruments that have strings?
2 People who review new music are called ....
3 Can you name five different types of music?
4 A person who works behind the scenes to make a band successful is called a music ....
5 The words of a song are called ....
6 The music of a song on an album is called a ....
7 Another word for the rhythm of a piece of music is called the ....
8 The people who really like a particular band are called ....

 Now go to Practice Extra Unit 3

Revision

UNIT 4

1 Choose the correct modal verb (A, B or C) to complete the sentences.

1 You .... always check your details when buying something online.
   A ought   B should   C have to
2 You .... go to the party, but only if you clean your room first.
   A can   B must   C should
3 Her brother dropped her computer so she .... to do the homework again because she didn't save it to the cloud.
   A must   B will have   C can
4 I .... wake up at 5.30 a.m. yesterday because the bus was leaving at 6.30 a.m.
   A could   B should   C had to
5 You .... scored if you hadn't slipped at the last minute!
   A should have   B could have   C must have
6 You .... worked really hard to have done so well on the test.
   A must have   B ought to have   C could have
7 You .... asked me if I wanted to go to the party before telling Peter I would come.
   A needn't have   B should have   C must have
8 He .... eat that cake – he's allergic to nuts.
   A doesn't have to   B needn't   C mustn't

2 Complete these sentences with a preposition in each gap.

1 My brother has become extremely successful, but I'm not jealous .... him at all.
2 You need to think .... which subjects you want to carry on studying next year.
3 When I get home, I like to talk .... my parents about my day at school.
4 I'm not very interested .... science, but I like the lessons when we do experiments.
5 Where we go for a holiday depends .... the cost of the accommodation.
6 When you go on the school trip you are responsible .... your belongings, so don't leave anything on the bus.
7 We're moving house next week; could you help .... the packing?
8 I'm really nervous .... taking part in the international basketball competition next week.
9 Some people look for things to complain .... all the time.
10 Cold winters with a lot of snow are typical .... Canada.

3 Complete the paragraph below with words from the box. Add *s* or *'s* if necessary. There is one extra word.

| defender   goalkeeper   penalty |
| pitch   referee   tackle |

A football match is always played on a (1) .... with a (2) .... making sure the players on both teams play fairly. On each team, it's the attacker's role to score goals and the (3) .... job to keep them out of the goal, with help from two or three (4) .... All the players try to (5) .... the opposition in order to get the ball.

4 Complete the lists with the correct form of each word.

Adjective	Noun
1 convenient	....
2 equal	....
3	generosity
4 independent	....
5	patience

Verb	Noun
6 conclude	....
7 connect	....
8	division
9 expand	....
10	persuasion

 Now go to Practice Extra Unit 4

Revision

UNIT 5

1 Match the two halves of the conditional sentences and put the verbs into the correct tense.

1 I might have liked the school science fair more
2 If he hadn't learnt to play the piano,
3 Unless you live very far away,
4 Take an umbrella with you
5 If I could change something about my school,
6 She won't have a packed lunch
7 Most people will never see a rhino
8 I'll go shopping with you
9 Sam said he would try to learn German
10 I feel terrible, and I can be quite grumpy in the mornings

a if they .... (start) teaching it at school.
b as long as you .... (buy) me a sandwich!
c unless they .... (go) to a big zoo.
d in case it .... (start) to rain.
e it .... (be) a good idea to cycle to school every day.
f if I .... (not get) enough sleep.
g he .... (miss out) on having such a creative career.
h unless she .... (prepare) it the night before.
i if there .... (be) more interactive displays, not just informative posters.
j it .... (be) the time it starts.

2 Complete the text with the correct form of the words in brackets.

Education in Britain

In Britain, children move to a **(1)** .... (SECOND) school at the age of 11. The vast **(2)** .... (MAJOR) of students go to a state school rather than a private one. There is no **(3)** .... (EXAMINE) you have to pass to get in, and this type of mixed-ability school is known as a **(4)** .... (COMPREHEND) school. However, students are divided into different groups according to their **(5)** .... (ABLE), a system known as streaming. The most able students go into the top set, where the most **(6)** .... (CHALLENGE) work is done. All the students study a **(7)** .... (VARY) of subjects, including English, maths and science, and also have the **(8)** .... (POSSIBLE) of doing sport, art and music as part of their timetable. At the age of 16, students have the **(9)** .... (CHOOSE) of which subjects to continue for the next two years, and at 18, those who want to go on to university put in their **(10)** .... (APPLY).

3 Complete the sentences with the words from the box.

| in   on   out x2   up x2 |

1 Everyone is very welcoming at my new school; whenever I have a question there is always somebody willing to help me ....
2 I missed .... on a lot of hockey training sessions because I broke my ankle.
3 My class put .... a show to raise money to fix the roof in the local theatre.
4 When she lived in Spain she picked .... a lot of the language.
5 Although we gave him plenty of encouragement, he wouldn't join .... with the song.
6 I know you said you're sorry, but it doesn't make .... for what you did.

 Now go to Practice Extra Unit 5

Revision

UNIT 6

1 Complete the text with *a*, *an* or *the*, or leave a gap if necessary.

Cape Town has **(1)** .... Mediterranean climate, with **(2)** .... mild, wet winters, and **(3)** .... dry and very warm summers. In winter, which lasts from **(4)** .... beginning of June to **(5)** .... end of August, **(6)** .... cold weather comes across from **(7)** .... Atlantic Ocean bringing **(8)** .... heavy rain and strong winds. **(9)** .... winter months are cool, with **(10)** .... minimum temperature of 7 °C (45 °F). Most of **(11)** .... city's annual rainfall occurs in wintertime, but rainfall amounts for **(12)** .... different suburbs can vary dramatically. Summer, which lasts from **(13)** .... November to March, is warm and dry. Cape Town gets frequent strong winds from **(14)** .... south-east, known locally as the Cape Doctor, because they blow away **(15)** .... pollution and clean **(16)** .... air in the city. However, Cape Town can be uncomfortably hot when the berg wind blows for **(17)** .... couple of weeks in February or early March. **(18)** .... Cape Town's weather is in fact remarkably similar to that of San Francisco in **(19)** .... USA, although it is definitely warmer, with **(20)** .... average air temperature of 19 °C (66 °F) versus San Francisco's 13 °C (55 °F).

2 Correct the mistakes in these sentences that exam candidates often make.

1 I've never seen so a beautiful garden.
2 It was my first experience of the theatre and I was such excited that I could hardly wait.
3 Sarah had never stayed in a hotel which was such beautiful like this.
4 The film was such a good that I could have watched it twice.
5 We picked such marvellous day to have a picnic.
6 I've never had a such tasty stew before.
7 I have so good memories from my childhood.
8 We had so a good time the last time we had dinner together.
9 I love going on holidays and travelling is such important to me.
10 I had never scored a such great goal before.

3 Complete these short expressions by writing a word from the box below.

> attachment   bags   conditioning
> equipment   ingredients   meals   paper
> produce   a shower   waste

1 air ....
2 electrical ....
3 email ....
4 fresh ....
5 local ....
6 plastic ....
7 ready ....
8 recycled ....
9 reduce ....
10 take ....

4 Now complete this text with the expressions from Exercise 3.

> If you want to live in an environmentally friendly way, there are lots of simple, practical steps you can take in your everyday life.

First of all, get your family to understand that it's important to **(1)** .... at home by cutting your energy consumption whenever possible. For instance, you can **(2)** .... rather than a bath, and always ensure that you turn off **(3)** .... when you have finished with it. Never leave the television or computer on standby! And if you use the computer a lot, use **(4)** .... for printing, and if at all possible send your homework by **(5)** .... instead of using paper. In addition, you should try to keep use of **(6)** .... in the home and family car to a minimum, even when it's very hot.

Remember too that you don't need **(7)** .... to take your shopping home when you go to the supermarket; it's much better to take a basket or box with you. When you're shopping for food, look for **(8)** .... rather than food that has been transported from miles away. Finally, if your family commits to healthy eating and you always prepare meals with **(9)** .... , you can avoid the huge amounts of packaging used to wrap the **(10)** .... you can find on the chilled counter.

 Now go to Practice Extra Unit 6

Revision

UNIT 7

1 Complete the sentences with the words from the box.

> brand   consumer   green product   imported goods
> sale item   vintage clothing

1 A .... is designed to protect the environment.
2 .... is produced in the past, and typical of the period in which it was made.
3 A .... is sold at a lower price than usual.
4 .... are products that come from another country.
5 A person who buys goods or services for their own use is a ....
6 Another word for a type of product made by a particular company is a ....

2 Complete the sentences with the words from the box.

> amused   anxious   astonished
> concerned   furious   irritated

1 I know you're only joking, but I'm not ....
2 She was getting more and more .... because the boy sat behind her on the flight kept kicking her seat.
3 I'm more than angry, I'm ....!
4 I couldn't believe what a bargain those shoes were. I was absolutely ....
5 He hasn't replied to any of my messages, so I'm starting to feel a little ....
6 I didn't sleep very well last night because I was so .... about the test.

3 Choose the correct form of the verbs.

> I arranged **(1) to go / going** away at the weekend with my friends, to a cabin in the woods. It wasn't a long journey but I still managed **(2) to fall / falling** asleep on the way because the car was so hot. My friend Laura had hoped **(3) to do / doing** the whole journey without stopping, but we took a break by a lake halfway there to cool down. Luckily, I had suggested **(4) to take / taking** our swimming things in case we felt like **(5) to swim / swimming**. We enjoyed **(6) to relax / relaxing** by the water for an hour or two and then we carried on **(7) to drive / driving**. When we arrived at the cabin, Laura tried **(8) to find / finding** the key in her backpack but it wasn't there. She said she remembered **(9) to put / putting** it in, and she made us **(10) to go / go** through all the other bags. In the end, we had to give up **(11) to look / looking** because it was getting dark. We had to choose between sleeping on the grass or going home, so we decided **(12) to go / going** home. At least we had a nice swim in the lake!

4 Complete the second sentence so that it has a similar meaning to the first sentence, using the word given. Do not change the word given. You must use between two and five words, including the word given.

1 James said, 'I can't play football because I'm looking after my brother.'
   EXPLAINED
   James .... play football because he was looking after his brother.

2 Alice said, 'OK, I'll help you with your maths homework.'
   AGREED
   Alice .... me with my maths homework.

3 My friend said he couldn't come with us to the cinema because he'd forgotten his money.
   SO
   My friend said, 'I've forgotten my money, ... with you to the cinema.'

4 My uncle said, 'This is the best show I've seen for years.'
   SUCH
   My uncle said he .... good show for years.

5 Anna said, 'I like your new dress.'
   TOLD
   Anna .... my new dress.

6 Archie asked me, 'Do you know how to play chess?'
   IF
   Archie asked me .... how to play chess.

 Now go to Practice Extra Unit 7

Revision

UNIT 8

1 Complete the text with *who*, *which*, *whose* or *where*. When you have finished, go back and add *that* or – (nothing) to those gaps where they are possible.

Edwin Hubble, **(1)** .... was born in 1889, was an American astronomer **(2)** .... work has made a huge contribution to what we know about the universe. There is a telescope, an asteroid and a moon crater **(3)** .... are all named after him. As a child, Hubble was someone **(4)** .... was both a bright student and an excellent athlete. He went to the University of Chicago, **(5)** .... he studied mathematics, astronomy and philosophy. He spent most of his working life in California, **(6)** .... he formulated Hubble's Law, **(7)** .... helped astronomers determine the age of the universe and prove that it was expanding. At the time, astronomers knew only about the Milky Way, a galaxy of stars and planets **(8)** .... the Earth is part of. But with Hubble's work it became clear that there were many more galaxies beyond the Milky Way.

2 Match the definitions with the scientific subjects.

1 The study of using scientific principles to design and build machines, structures and other things.
2 The study of treating illness or injury.
3 The study of relationships between air, land, water, animals and plants.
4 The study of substances and how they react.
5 The study of the universe and of objects that exist naturally in space.
6 The study of electric current and technology that uses it.

a chemistry
b astronomy
c medicine
d electronics
e engineering
f ecology

3 Complete the sentences with the correct form of the word in capitals at the end of each sentence.

1 If you go to the gym a lot, you will really build up your ....
STRONG
2 Young people didn't attend the town festival last year – we need to make it more .... to them.
ATTRACT
3 Our house was .... an old barn, but my family converted it.
ORIGINAL
4 We couldn't decide what food to buy as there were too many .... to choose from.
POSSIBLE
5 When he didn't turn up on Friday I was really cross, but it was just a .... ; he thought we'd agreed to meet on Saturday.
UNDERSTAND
6 If you support your ideas with facts you can make a more .... argument.
POWER
7 I prefer to pay for a streaming service to watch TV shows, to avoid all of the ....
COMMERCE
8 It's .... to start eating before everyone has sat down at the table.
POLITE

 Now go to Practice Extra Unit 8

REVISION 77

Visual materials

UNIT 3
Page 25, Speaking Part 2

Student A

Why might people enjoy singing in these different ways?

Visual materials

UNIT 3
Page 25, Speaking Part 2

Student B

Why do you think people want to watch these different types of theatre performance?

VISUAL MATERIALS 79

Visual materials

UNIT 5
Page 44, Speaking Part 2

Candidate B: Look at photographs 3 and 4. Compare them and answer the question. Tell your answer to Candidate A. Use these phrases if you are not sure about what you see in the photos:
it may/might/could be a … it looks like a … it's similar to a … it's a sort of …

Candidate A: When Candidate B has finished, discuss together which lesson you would prefer to do and why. Give reasons. Here are some phrases you can use:
I'd rather … because it's more interesting. It's good to learn something new. I'd rather be outside. I don't like/enjoy doing … because …

What do you think the pupils will learn on their visits?

Grammar reference

UNIT 1

Present tenses

We use the present simple
1 to say when things happen if they take place regularly:
   I **meet** my friends on Saturdays.
2 to talk about permanent situations:
   I **live** in a small flat.
3 to state general truths:
   Teenagers **sleep** more than adults.

We use the present continuous
1 to talk about the present moment:
   Go away – I**'m watching** TV.
2 for a temporary action or event:
   I**'m staying** with my granny for a couple of days.
3 for repeated actions and events over a period of time:
   I**'m learning** to play the guitar. (but not exactly at the present moment)
4 for changing or developing situations:
   The world **is getting** warmer.

State verbs

These are generally used in a simple tense (i.e. not a continuous tense). They are mostly about thoughts, feelings, belonging and the senses. Here are some common examples:
believe, know, mean, remember, suppose, understand, feel (= believe), think (= believe), adore, despise, hate, like, love, want, wish, prefer, belong, have / have got (= possess), own, smell, taste, hear, see, feel (= experience something physical or emotional), contain, seem, look (= seem), weigh

I **like** our new flat.
I **have** three sisters.

Present tenses in future clauses

In clauses referring to future time and which begin with when, until, before, after, as soon as, we use the present simple:

I'll call you when I **get** to my friend's. (**not** … when I will get)
Or the present perfect:
I'll have dinner when I**'ve finished** my homework. (**not** … when I will have finished)

The future

We use the present simple for scheduled events with a future meaning:
The bus **leaves** for London at 8.15 on Saturday.
We use the present continuous for plans which are already arranged:

We're **playing** football on Wednesday.
We use will
1 for decisions made at the moment of speaking:
   The phone's ringing. I**'ll answer** it.
2 for anything which is uncertain, especially with probably, maybe, I think, I hope and I expect:
   I probably **won't finish** this project today.
3 for predictions (as they are not definite):
   The number of people on the planet **will grow** to nine billion by 2050.
4 for requests, promises, offers:
   I**'ll give** you your book back on Friday.

We use going to
1 for something we have decided to do but which isn't a definite arrangement:
   I**'m going to ring** my friend in a minute.
2 to predict something when we have some evidence:
   It**'s going to rain**. (I can see the clouds.)
   We can often use either the present continuous or going to for plans:
   I**'m meeting** / I**'m going to meet** my friends in town.
   We use the future continuous for an event happening at a particular time or over a period of time in the future:
   I can't come at 6.00 as I**'ll be looking** after my sister.

1 Choose the correct options to complete the text. Sometimes there may be more than one possible answer.

Many people **(1) take up / are taking up** running these days. Running is great because it **(2) helps / is helping** our general fitness. When we run, we **(3) use up / are using up** more energy than when we **(4) walk / are walking**. I **(5) go / am going** running regularly, and I like to run after school to help me relax. At the moment, I **(6) train / 'm training** for a race, so I **(7) spend / 'm spending** a lot of time out running.

2 Complete the sentences with either the present simple or the present continuous form of the verbs in brackets.

1 I .... for a long walk three times a week after school. (go)
2 I .... my friend Max at the cinema tonight. (meet)
3 It really annoys me when people .... to my messages. (not reply)
4 Cycling .... a more popular way to travel around cities. (become)
5 Can you call back later? Fred .... his dad in the garden at the moment. (help)
6 I'll order a takeaway for dinner. .... you .... Indian food or Chinese food? (prefer)

GRAMMAR REFERENCE 81

Comparisons

1 syllable (*warm*)	2 syllables ending in -*y* (*happy*)	2 or more syllables (*expensive*)
warmer (than)	happier (than)	more expensive (than)
(the) warmest	(the) happiest	the most expensive

Some two-syllable adjectives (e.g. *quiet, polite*) and adjectives ending in -*ow*, -*er* and -*le* can take both forms:
Jo is **more polite** than Sam. = Jo is **politer** than Sam.
Irregular adjectives:
good, better, best
bad, worse, worst
far, farther/further, farthest/furthest

We use comparative structures to compare people or things

1 with an adjective:
My brother is **taller than** my sister.
My sister **isn't as tall as** my brother.
I'm **as good** at football **as** my older brother.
This TV programme is **less interesting than** last week's.

2 with a noun:
I get **more/less pocket money** than you.

3 Put the words in order to make sentences with the comparative or superlative.

1 Her musical talent / than / has always / her sister's. / greater / been
2 were as impressive / the scores / His results / the competition / as / of his nearest rival. / throughout
3 The lecturer is / since he started / less / attending conferences / available to his students / every month.
4 The plants / are not / as fast / as my friends predicted. / growing
5 Her interest in / considerably / than / history is / greater now / it was / at the beginning of her degree.
6 ideally want. / close to them / Their daughter doesn't live / as / quite / as they would
7 than / There are slightly / living in / more people / five years ago. / the village
8 more / than by plane. / It's / to travel by train / considerably / environmentally friendly

UNIT 2

Adverb formation

Many adverbs are formed from adjectives by adding the suffix -*ly*, but note the following:
Adjectives ending in -*y* change their last letter to -*i* before adding -*ly*: *angry* → *angrily*

Adjectives ending in consonant + -*le* lose the last letter before adding -*ly*: *probable* → *probably*
Adjectives ending in -*e* keep the -*e* and add -*ly*: *rare* → *rarely*
Adjectives ending in -*l* add -*ly*: *careful* → *carefully*
Adverbs never go between the verb and its object.
He washed his car **carefully**. (**not** ~~He washed carefully his car.~~)

1 Tick (✓) the correct sentences. Correct the sentences with mistakes.

1 Hopefully, we will all pass our exams and be able to celebrate at the end of the year.
2 The teacher explained quickly the task to the students.
3 The little girl signed her name beautifully on the picture she had drawn.
4 Unfortunately, many people don't understand the importance of eating a healthy diet.
5 Susan sang happily her favourite song as she got ready to go out.
6 The children devoured the meal hungrily.

Past tenses

We use the past simple for

1 completed actions and events in the past:
I **went** to the city centre yesterday.
2 repeated actions and events in the past:
I **practised** the guitar every day before the concert. (But the concert's over now so I don't practise every day.)
3 permanent or long-term situations in the past:
My family **lived** in Paris for four years. (But they don't now.)

We use the present perfect simple

1 to talk about a period of time which is still continuing, sometimes with *since* or *for*:
I**'ve lived** in this village **for five** years. (And I continue to live here.)
2 for unfinished actions and events, sometimes with *still* or *yet*:
I **haven't been** to the new pool **yet**. (But I hope I will go there.)
3 for events that happened in the recent past, sometimes with *just*:
She**'s (just) gone** to the cinema. (And she's still there.)
4 to talk about how many times something has happened, sometimes with *already*:
I**'ve (already) heard** this band several times.

We use the present perfect continuous (often with *since* or *for*) when we want to emphasise the activity rather than the result.

Compare:

I've been reading this book for weeks. (I still haven't finished it.)
I've read four books this week. (I've finished them.)
I've been doing my homework while you've been out. (That's how I spent the time.)
I've done my homework while you've been out. (I've finished it.)

We use the past continuous
1 to talk about a particular moment in the past:
I **was listening** to the radio at 8.30 this morning.
2 for an activity beginning before a past action (usually in the past simple) and continuing until or after it:
I **was going** upstairs when I **heard** a strange noise.
3 for two things happening at the same time:
It **was pouring** with rain while **we were** playing football.

We use the past perfect simple
1 to refer to an earlier time when we are already talking about the past, often with time expressions like *when*, *after*, *by the time*, *as soon as*:
By the time I was six, I**'d lived** in three different places.
2 with adverbs like *just*, *already*, *before*, *ever* and *never*:
Jasmine offered to lend me her book but I**'d already finished** my homework.

We use *used to* and *would* to talk about past habits when we are emphasising they are no longer true. *Used to* is more common than *would*:
My mum **used to sing** to me every night.
= My mum **would sing** to me every night.

Used to can describe actions and states, but *would* can only describe actions:
My brother used to live in Sydney. (**not** My brother would live …)

2 Choose the correct options to complete the sentences.
1 While I **listened / was listening** to music, my brother was playing in the garden.
2 My friends **often phoned / were often phoning** me in the evenings.
3 While I was baking a cake, I **realised / was realising** that the recipe was wrong.
4 It was a beautiful day. The sun **shone / was shining** and the birds **sang / were singing**.
5 Sky Brown **won / was winning** a bronze medal for Britain at the Tokyo Olympics.

3 Complete the sentences with the past simple or past continuous form of the verbs in brackets.
1 While I .... (pack) for my holiday, I .... (find) some old sunglasses.
2 As I .... (leave) the restaurant, I .... (realise) that I'd left my scarf behind.
3 While Mark .... (practise) the piano, his sister .... (watch) TV.
4 When we .... (hear) the protests, we all .... (stop) what we .... (do) and .... (look) out of the window.
5 My computer .... (crash) while I .... (write) my essay.

4 Complete the sentences with the past perfect simple or continuous form of the verbs in brackets.
1 We were furious, because we .... (wait) for over two hours before the train arrived at the station.
2 She .... (write) poetry for over three years before she finally decided to try to get some of her poems published.
3 Martha's family devoured the cake that she .... (bake) only an hour before.
4 I must have dropped the letter that she .... (hand) to me.
5 When they got home, they discovered that their babysitter .... (already read) their toddler a bedtime story.
6 When I finally reached the front of the queue, I found out that my sister .... (pick up) the tickets an hour earlier.

5 Complete the sentences with the past perfect simple or continuous form of the verbs in brackets.
1 The waiter, who was under a lot of pressure, brought a starter that I .... (not order).
2 I had great difficulty recalling the poem I .... (try) to memorise the previous night.
3 The children excitedly collected the fruit that .... (fall) from the trees.
4 She .... (play) tennis all afternoon when we saw her briefly as we walked past the park.
5 I .... (read) a chapter of my book every evening for over two weeks, so I was upset when I forgot to take my book with me on holiday.
6 He .... (live) in Paris all his life and was reluctant to move, even when he was offered a place at a top university.

6 Complete the sentences with the correct form of *used to* and the verbs in brackets.

1 I .... eating spinach when I was a child, but now I love it! (– / enjoy)
2 Her friend .... judo, but now she trains twice a week. (– / do)
3 They .... hours playing football in the park. (+ / spend)
4 My mother .... a beautiful grand piano. (+ / own)
5 .... she .... in touch with her relatives before they emigrated to New Zealand? (? / keep)
6 I .... the sound of fireworks when I was young. (– / like)

7 Tick (✓) the correct sentences. Correct the sentences with mistakes.

1 My dad would play in a band every weekend before he got married.
2 I would work in a hotel for many years in my youth.
3 When she was younger, she would enjoy playing the flute and would practise every day.
4 I would live in London near Hyde Park until I left to go to university in Nottingham.
5 When I was a kid I would play in the park with my friends until it was quite dark and my mother called me to go in.
6 I didn't use to enjoy the taste of seafood, until I had the chance to eat some fresh mussels in Scotland last year.

UNIT 3

Linking words and phrases

We use *in spite of*, *despite*, *although*, *even though*, *but*, *however* and *while* to contrast two ideas or events.

Despite and *in spite of* are prepositions; they are followed by *-ing*, a noun or by *the fact that* + subject + verb:

The singer finished the show **despite having** a sore throat.
They continued filming **despite the bad weather**.
The concert was a success **in spite of the fact that** the guitarist was new.

Although and *even though* are conjunctions; they are followed by a noun/pronoun and a verb:

They continued filming **although** / **even though** the weather was bad.
She never sings her own songs **although** / **even though** she's written a lot.

But and *however* have the same meaning. *But* joins two halves of a sentence. *However* contrasts two separate sentences and is more formal than *but*:

He is a really good actor **but** I didn't enjoy his latest film.
He is a really good actor. **However**, I didn't enjoy his latest film.
He is a really good actor. I didn't, **however**, enjoy his latest film.

While can go at the beginning or in the middle of a sentence:

While I know he's a very good writer, I still don't like his books.
Annie has dark hair and eyes **while** her brother has fair hair and blue eyes.

1 Tick (✓) the correct sentences. Correct the sentences with mistakes.

1 Michael didn't get a sports scholarship. Even though he's really good at basketball.
2 Despite he had an injury last year, Scott was able to compete in the world championships.
3 In spite of we left the house really early, we still missed our flight.
4 Fran really enjoyed the summer camp, although it rained most days.
5 In spite of the fact that she practised every day, she didn't pass her driving test.

The passive

Active	Passive
Kai **plays** lead guitar.	Lead guitar **is played** by Kai.
The DJ **is playing** my favourite song now.	My favourite song **is being played** by the DJ now.
The band first **recorded** this song in 2009.	This song **was** first **recorded** by the band in 2009.
Lots of different people **have sung** this song.	This song **has been sung** by lots of different people.
You **can download** the track for free.	The track **can be downloaded** for free.
The band's fans **will buy** their new album.	Their new album **will be bought** by the band's fans.
The shops **had sold** a million copies of the album by midday.	A million copies of the album **had been sold** by midday.

The passive is used when

1 we don't know who or what does/did something:
*My bike **was stolen** from outside the school.*
2 the action is more important than who does/did it:
*The match **has been cancelled** because of the weather.*
3 it is obvious who or what does/did something:
*The film **will be shot** in Brazil.*

We can use *by* + person/thing to show who does/did the action if this is important information:
*This song **was written** by Chris Martin.*

Verbs with two objects in the passive

There are two ways of making the passive of verbs that take two objects (e.g. *give, show, tell*):
*The boy band **was given** first prize.*
*First prize **was given** to the boy band.*

have something done

We use the structure *have* + thing/person + past participle when someone else does something for us:
*She **had** her hair and make-up **done** before going on the stage.*

2 Choose the correct option (A, B or C) to complete the sentences.

1 The old paintings .... by expert art historians.
  A were restored
  B was restored
  C been restored
2 My handbag with my money and phone .... at the railway station.
  A been stolen
  B were stolen
  C was stolen
3 The woman in the photograph .... for questioning by the police.
  A had wanted
  B gets wanted
  C is wanted
4 Your theatre tickets .... and you can collect them from the box office on the day of the show.
  A had been reserved
  B have been reserved
  C have reserved
5 The roof of their house .... badly damaged in the storm.
  A been
  B had
  C got
6 They .... for fraud.
  A were arrested
  B been arrested
  C arrested

UNIT 4

Modal verbs

Ability

We use *can* or *be able to* to say someone has an ability:
*My brother **can** cook but he's very bad at washing up.*

We use *could* or *was able to* to say someone had an ability:
*I **could speak** two languages when I was little.*

In all other tenses, we use a form of *be able to* to talk about ability:
*I **won't be able to come** skiing because I've hurt my foot.*

1 Complete the sentences with a modal verb from the box. One of the modal verbs is used twice.

| can   can't   could   couldn't   was able to |

1 .... you ride a bike when you were five?
2 He .... get to the party on time yesterday, because his dad's car broke down.
3 He's absolutely amazing – he's only seven and he .... speak five languages, including Greek.
4 She was relieved, because she .... find a taxi and get to the airport on time.
5 I've searched everywhere for my glasses, but I .... find them anywhere.
6 I .... lift this box – it's so heavy! Could you help me, please?

2 Tick (✓) the correct sentences. Correct the sentences with mistakes.

1 I wasn't able translate the text into German, because it contained too many unfamiliar expressions.
2 When the waiter showed me the bill for my meal, I didn't have enough money on me to pay for it, but fortunately I could use my emergency credit card this time.
3 Thank you for your offer to lend me some money, but I am afraid I couldn't accept it.
4 When you finally move into your new bedroom, you'll be able to decorate it as you wish.
5 I could taste and smell the onions for hours after the meal.
6 She could run the marathon in less than three hours, although she had not been training regularly for ten days.

Permission and advice

We use *can* to mean 'it is possible' or 'it is allowed':
You **can borrow** my tennis racket if you want.
When we are talking about the right thing to do, we use *should(n't)* or *ought (not) to*:
You **should tell** your parents where you are going.

Expectations

When we expect something to happen, we use *should (not)*:
Our team **should do** well today as we've practised so much.
We also use *should* when we discover a situation is not as we expected it:
My phone **should be** in my pocket because that's where I left it.
In the past, we say *should(n't) have*:
We **should have scored** more goals as we had lots of chances.

3 Find and correct the mistake in each sentence below.
1 She shouldn't have ate all those crisps.
2 They should arrived by now.
3 I should have listen to my friend's advice.
4 People ought waste less food.
5 You should to ask your teacher for help if you don't understand the question.

Obligation

We can often use either *must* or *have to* with the same meaning:
I **must** / **have to phone** my mum now.
We use *must* to give orders or strong advice, including to ourselves:
I **must remember** to bring my football boots tomorrow.
You **must** try harder.
When there is a rule or where the obligation does not come from the speaker, *must* is possible but *have to* is more usual:
We **have to be** at football practice early tomorrow.
We normally use *have to* for habits:
I **have to practise** every day.
We only use *must* in the present tense. In all other tenses, we use *have to*:
I **had to buy** new football boots because my feet had grown.
We**'ll have to find** a new goalkeeper because Matt is ill.

Although *must* and *have to* both express obligation, *mustn't* and *don't have to* have different meanings:
You **mustn't wear** shoes in the gym. (Don't do it.)
We also say *You can't* or *You're not allowed to*.
We use *don't have to* when there is **no** obligation to do something:
I **don't have to take** any money because the bus is free. (It's not necessary to do it.)
We can also say *You don't need to* or *You needn't*.

Certainty and possibility

In the present we use

1 *must* when we are sure something is true:
 Those boots **must belong** to Cameron. He's got big feet.
2 *can't/couldn't* when we are sure something is not true:
 That **can't be** Sara because she doesn't come to this school any more.
3 *might/may/could* when we think something is possible:
 This text **might be** from Dan but it doesn't say.
4 *might not / may not* when we think something is uncertain:
 I'll phone him but he **might not be** there.

Could means the same as *may/might* (something is possible) but *couldn't* means something is not true, which is different from *may not/might not* (something is uncertain).

In the past we use

1 *must have* when we are sure something is true:
 Ava's coat isn't here so she **must have gone** home.
2 *can't/couldn't have* when we are sure something is not true:
 Claire's coat is here so she **can't/couldn't have gone** home.
3 *might/may/could have* when we think something is possible:
 Adam **might have borrowed** my bike because it's not here and his is broken.
 Luca isn't here. He **might/may/could have forgotten** to come because we changed the day.
4 *might/may not have* when we think something is uncertain:
 You **might/may not have heard** Ellie's good news because you weren't here yesterday.

Could have means the same as *may/might have* (something is possible) but *couldn't have* means something is not true, which is different from *may/might not have* (something is uncertain).

4 Choose the correct options to complete the sentences.

1 If you don't pay attention to your skiing instructor, you **could / can** have an accident.
2 You **can't have / might have** passed the maths test because you didn't do any revision!
3 Do we **have to / must** get up now?
4 I **must / have** try to argue less often with my younger brother.
5 The police warned me that I **can / must** never drive without insurance again.
6 When I was a child, people **couldn't / mustn't** access the internet with their mobile phones.
7 We **didn't need to / must** queue to get into the concert because we got to the venue really early.
8 You **can / must** buy lunch in the canteen or bring a sandwich if you prefer.

Prepositions: *at, in, on*

At

We use *at*

- when we think of a place as a point, not an area (including at home, at school, at work, at university):
  The delivery man is **at** the back door.
  The cars were waiting **at** the barrier.
- to talk about an event with a number of people:
  We'll both be **at** the reception this evening.
  The students were **at** the seminar about virtual reality.

In

We use *in*

- when we think of a place as an area or space:
  He had his workshop **in** the basement of his house.
  The headquarters of the company are located **in** Silicon Valley.
  Many British criminals try to escape the law by living **in** villas in the south of Spain.
- for cars and taxis:
  He spent two hours **in** a taxi because of the rush hour.
  I keep up to date with the news by listening to the radio **in** the car.
- normally with *in class, in hospital, in prison, in court*:
  My partner is still **in** hospital after the accident in the warehouse at work.
  He defended his client **in** court.

- with people or things which form lines:
  She was prepared to wait **in** a queue for hours for a bargain.
- for the world:
  There's a lot of competition between Dubai and Saudi Arabia to construct the tallest building **in** the world.

On

We use *on*

- to talk about a position in contact with a surface:
  They posted announcements **on** the walls of the building.
  The frying pan is **on** the cooker.
  She was relaxing **on** the terrace all afternoon.
- with *border, coast, road to, the outskirts of, the edge of, the way to/from*, etc:
  On the border between France and Germany, there was a bakery selling typical bread and pastry.
- with means of transport apart from cars and taxis:
  The wind demolished the sail **on** our yacht.
- for technology:
  He denies that he spends hours **on** the phone.
  I rediscovered a friend from school **on** Facebook.
- with *left* and *right*:
  There was a sharp bend in the road **on** the left.
  Can you see the man in shorts leaning against the door over there **on** your right?

5 Choose the correct preposition in italics.

1 There are lots of fortified castles **on / in / at** the border between Spain and Portugal.
2 A lot of children are failing to achieve at school because they are spending too much time **on / in / at** their phones.
3 He damaged his car quite badly because he didn't see the vehicle parked **on / in / at** the left until too late.
4 I saw several old friends and acquaintances **on / in / at** the festival.
5 I didn't set out early enough and got stuck **on / in / at** a traffic jam **on / in / at** the M25 ring road.
6 The last time I saw that talented young actor was on the stage **on / in / at** the Royal Shakespeare Theatre.

UNIT 5

Conditionals

- *If* + present simple, + present simple
  We use the zero conditional to state general facts and truths:
  Children **do** better at school **if** they **sleep** well. (This is a known fact.)

If children **sleep** well, they **do** better at school.

- *If* + present simple, + *will/modal* + infinitive

  We use the first conditional for a future condition which we believe is possible or likely:

  If you **give** me some money, I**'ll buy** a ticket for you.

  If you **chat** to your friends during lessons, you **won't learn** anything.

  I **can cycle** to school tomorrow *if* I **feel** better. (I think I will feel better.)

- *If* + past simple, + *would/could* + infinitive

  We use the second conditional for an imaginary condition which we believe to be impossible or unlikely. We use the past tense although the speaker is thinking about the present or the future:

  You **could win** first prize *if* you **practised** more.

  I **could reach** that shelf *if* I **were** taller. (But I'm not taller so I can't reach.)

  We can use *were* or *was* after *if I/he/she/it*.

  Compare the first and second conditionals:

  If you **spent** more time on your homework, you **would get** better marks. (But you almost certainly won't spend more time.)

  If you **spend** more time on your homework, you**'ll get** better marks. (more likely)

- *If* + past perfect, + *would/could/might have* + past participle

  We use the third conditional to talk about past events which cannot be changed, so we know the condition is impossible:

  If my dad **hadn't driven** me to school, I **would have been** late. (But he drove me so I wasn't late.)

  My friend **would have been** upset *if* I**'d forgotten** her birthday. (But she wasn't upset because I didn't forget.)

  We sometimes see sentences which contain a mixture of second and third conditionals because of their context:

  I **wouldn't have lost** my purse *if* I **were** more careful. (I did lose it because I am generally not very careful.)

  Compare: I **wouldn't have lost** my purse *if* I **had been** more careful. (On this particular occasion I wasn't careful.)

  We can start conditional sentences with either the *if*-clause or the main clause. If we put the main clause first, there is no comma between the clauses:

  If you smiled more, you'd make friends.

  You'd make friends if you smiled more.

1 Complete the sentences with the first or second conditional form of the verbs in brackets.

1. If she .... (be) late, we .... (have to) leave without her.
2. If I .... (be) you, I .... (buy) that smartphone.
3. If you .... (come) this way, the teacher .... (see) you now.
4. If I .... (have) more time, I .... (not be) late for school yesterday.
5. Unless the weather .... (improve) significantly, we .... (have to) cancel the barbecue.
6. I .... (go) on a round-the-world holiday if I .... (win) the lottery.

2 Choose the correct verb tense (A, B or C).

1. If my sister .... to lend me some money, I wouldn't have bought that expensive gift.
   A didn't agree
   B doesn't agree
   C hadn't agreed
2. I wouldn't have gone on that guided tour if you .... it to me.
   A didn't recommend
   B don't recommend
   C hadn't recommended
3. He would have paid for his lunch if he .... his wallet at home.
   A wouldn't leave
   B didn't leave
   C hadn't left
4. If you .... for your teacher's support, she would have willingly helped you in any way she could.
   A had asked
   B asked
   C ask
5. I would have been extremely disappointed if you .... to the party.
   A don't come
   B hadn't come
   C wouldn't have come
6. If he .... rushing to get to the basketball match, he wouldn't have put on the wrong shoes.
   A wasn't
   B hadn't been
   C wouldn't be

3 Complete the third conditional sentences with the verbs in brackets.

1 If you .... (not / arrive) late at the train station, we .... (not / miss) our train to Newcastle.
2 If they .... (come) home from the party at a reasonable time, they .... (not / get up) so late.
3 If he .... (work) harder during his internship, he .... (might get) that amazing job as a journalist.
4 If you .... (be) born in Montreal, you probably .... (learn) to speak two languages.
5 If she .... (not board) that flight to Brazil, she .... (never meet) her best friend.
6 He .... (catch) a taxi from the airport if he .... (have) enough money.

Other ways of expressing *if*

Unless, in case, as/so long as, provided (that) / providing (that)

All these expressions are followed by the present tense even when we are talking about the future.

1 *Unless* means 'except if':
You'll get a ticket if you get in the queue early. = *You won't get a ticket **unless** you get in the queue early.*
2 We use *in case* when we do something because something else might happen:
*I'll tidy my room **in case** my friends want to go in there.* (I'll tidy it now before they come because they might want to go in there.)
In case doesn't have the same meaning as *if*:
*I'll tidy my room **if** my friends want to go in there.* (I won't tidy it before they come because they might not want to go in there.)
3 *As/So long as* and *provided (that) / providing (that)* can be used instead of *if* and mean 'only if' or 'on the condition that':
*I'll go to the party **as/so long as** you come too.*

I wish

To say we would like a present situation to be different, we use *I wish / if only* + past simple:
I wish I had my own bedroom. (But I don't.)
To say we want something to happen or someone (not) to do something, we use *I wish / if only* + *would* + infinitive:
***If only** the rain **would stop**.*
***I wish** my mum **would let** me stay up later.*
To say we would like a future situation to be different, we use *I wish / If only* + subject + *could* + infinitive:

*If only I **could** go on holiday.*
To express a wish or regret about the past we use *I wish / If only* + past perfect (it's like a third conditional):
*My mum wishes she **hadn't bought** this car.*
(Because it goes wrong all the time.)

4 Complete the sentences with verbs in the past simple, with *could* + infinitive or with *would* + infinitive.

1 I wish I .... (have) a really well-paid job in the media industry.
2 If only I .... (meet) some people who are adventurous like me.
3 I wish that dog outside .... (stop) barking. I'm getting a headache!
4 If only he .... (start) studying harder for his exams.
5 I wish I .... (have) more time to meet up with my friends last weekend.
6 If only my mother .... (not keep) asking me if I've tidied my room.

5 Choose the correct options to complete the sentences.

1 I wish I **would be** / **was** better at maths.
2 If only he **could stop** / **would stop** playing his drums so loudly when I'm trying to work.
3 If only I **knew** / **would know** how to drive a car.
4 I wish I **could play** / **would play** the piano better.
5 He wishes he **knew** / **could know** how to cook Indian food.
6 If only the dog **wouldn't roll** / **didn't roll** in the mud every time we went out.

UNIT 6

Countable and uncountable nouns

Nouns can be either countable, e.g. *bed, child, trip* or uncountable, e.g. *accommodation, advice, experience, homework, information, music, news, pollution*.
Some nouns can be both but with different meanings:
*These maths **exercises** are easy.* [C]
***Exercise** is good for you.* [U]

Countable nouns

1 can be singular and have *a/an* before them: *a cat, a job, an adventure*
2 can be plural (sometimes with *many/few/some* or a number before them): *some friends, many animals, three buses*

Uncountable nouns
1 cannot be plural: Take my advice. (**not** advices)
2 take a singular verb: This food **is** delicious.
3 can have *some/much/little* before them: *some bread, not much information, a little homework*
4 can use other words to refer to quantity: *a slice of bread, a piece of paper*

1 Tick (✓) the correct sentences. Correct the sentences with mistakes.
1 My friends and I finally found some suitable accommodations at a reasonable rent.
2 My brother was astonished to discover that the airline charged us extra for our luggages.
3 A pollution from traffic fumes can cause some people to get ill.
4 I usually reject an advice from my aunt.
5 The company's website had little information about prices and delivery dates.
6 All of the sculptures in the exhibition are extremely valuable work of art.

2 Choose the correct options to complete the sentences.
1 Many experts argue that it is not wise to drink **coffee / coffees** late in the evening.
2 Jack stayed in various types of **accommodations / accommodation** while he was travelling.
3 There's a container for recycling **cardboards / cardboard** and waste **papers / paper** behind our house.
4 Some of the news about the damage done by the floods **were / was** very upsetting.
5 The cost of the **equipment / equipments** needed to play ice hockey **is / are** beyond the reach of many people.
6 The engineers were desperately struggling to repair the **damages / damage** caused to the railway line by the storm.

Articles

A(n), the and no article
A(n) is used with singular countable nouns and introduces a new item of information:
*I have **an** idea.*

The is used with countable and uncountable nouns, for items mentioned before, or when the speaker and listener both know what they are talking about:
*There's **a** mouse in **the** kitchen.* (The mouse is new but the speaker and listener know which kitchen.)

We don't use an article with plural countable and uncountable nouns when we talk about things in a general sense. Compare:
***Musicians** don't earn much.* (musicians in general)
***Music** makes people feel better.* (music in general)
***The music** is too loud.* (this particular music which is playing now)

Special uses of articles
The is used with
- oceans, seas and rivers (*the Black Sea*, the *Thames*)
- regions (*the south of France, the Far East*)
- groups of islands (*the Philippines*)
- names of countries that include a word like *Republic, Kingdom* or *States* (*the United States*)
- deserts and mountain ranges (*the Alps, the Kalahari Desert*)

We don't use *the* with
- lakes (*Lake Garda*)
- continents, most countries, states, cities, towns and villages (*Europe, Florida, Rome*)
- buildings and locations which use a name (*John Lennon Airport, Edinburgh University*)
- names of countries that include a word like *Republic, Kingdom* or *States* (*the United States*)
- many common expressions: *by train/bus, at home, at work, in hospital, have lunch/dinner, watch television* (but *listen to the radio*)

3 Complete the sentences with definite or indefinite articles.

1 I heard .... loud noise in .... attic.
2 I think that .... man driving .... car is .... member of .... British royal family.
3 They are looking for .... apartment on .... outskirts of town.
4 What's .... tallest building in the world?
5 The government is building more affordable housing for .... poor.
6 She's .... tour guide in one of .... most beautiful towns in Austria.

So and such (a/an)

So and *such* are used for emphasis, often with a result clause.

So is followed by

1 an adjective:
   *Global warming is **so worrying**.*
   *The giraffes were **so tall** that you could see them above the trees.*
2 an adverb:
   *The lion came **so close** (that) everyone was scared.*
3 *much*, *many* and *few* with or without a noun:
   *There were **so many people** (that) we couldn't see.*
   *I ate **so much** (that) I could hardly move.*

Such is followed by

1 *a/an* (+ adjective) + singular noun: *It was **such a good film** (that) I wanted to watch it again.*
   *I had **such a surprise** when the doorbell rang.*
2 (adjective +) plural noun: *There were **such problems** (that) we had to cancel the trip.*
   *I had **such good results** in the test (that) my parents gave me a laptop.*
3 (adjective +) uncountable noun: *The trip was **such fun**.*
   *This is **such strong glass** (that) it will never break.*
4 *a lot / a lot of* + noun: *There was **such a lot** to tell my mum (that) I didn't know where to start.*
   *My uncle has **such a lot of money** (that) he doesn't know what to spend it on.*

4 Complete the sentences with *so* or *such* (*a / an*).

1 I was .... tired that I fell asleep on the train and missed my stop.
2 It was .... hot day that I sat in the shade.
3 Let's talk on the phone because I have .... much to tell you!
4 He gave the dog a treat because he was sat .... patiently.
5 It's .... difficult decision, I don't know what to do.

Too and enough

Enough means 'sufficient, the right quantity' and *too* means 'more than enough'. We use *too* and *enough* with adjectives, adverbs and nouns.

Enough goes

1 before a noun: *I've got **enough money**.*
2 after an adjective: *I'm not **old enough** to drive.*
3 after an adverb: *We didn't run **quickly enough**.*

Too goes

1 before *much/many* + a noun: *I've got **too much homework**.*
2 before an adjective: *I'm **too young** to drive.*
3 before an adverb: *He ran **too quickly** for us to catch him.*

5 Underline and correct the mistakes in these sentences.

1 Is the food enough hot?
2 I arrived too late catch my bus.
3 We have medicine enough for all the patients.
4 They aren't enough fit to play for the rugby team.
5 The room was enough dark to see anything.

UNIT 7

Verbs and expressions followed by *to* + infinitive or *-ing*

- Verb + *to* + infinitive, e.g. (*can't*) *afford, agree, aim, appear, arrange, attempt, decide, demand, deserve, fail, forget, hope, learn, manage, offer, plan, pretend, refuse, seem, tend,* (*can't*) *wait*:
  *You **deserve to do** well.*
  *She **pretended not to notice**.*

- Verb (+ object) + *to* + infinitive, e.g. *ask, choose, expect, help, intend, prepare, promise, want*:
  *We **expected** them **to wait** for us.*

- Verb + object + *to* + infinitive, e.g. *dare, encourage, force, invite, order, persuade, remind, teach, tell, warn*:
  *My friend **dared** me **to jump** across the river.*

- *Make* and *let* are followed by the infinitive without *to* and always have an object:
  *I **made my brother come** shopping with me.*

- Verbs followed by *-ing*, e.g. *avoid, can't help, can't stand, carry on, consider, delay, dislike, enjoy, feel like, finish, give up, imagine, involve, keep / keep on, mention,* (*not*) *mind, miss, postpone, practise, put off, suggest*:
  *I **suggested playing** badminton instead of tennis.*
  *I **enjoy not having** much to do on Sundays.*

GRAMMAR REFERENCE 91

- Verbs and expressions ending in a preposition always take -ing:

  I **gave up doing** gymnastics when I hurt my foot.
  I am **interested in becoming** a fashion designer.

- Some verbs can be followed by the *to* + infinitive or *-ing* but with a difference in meaning, e.g. *forget, go on, mean, remember, stop, try*:

  Remember to take your keys with you. (something you have to do)

  I **remember taking** my keys with me. (a memory of a past action)

  Try to walk faster. (attempt to do it if you can)

  Try taking more exercise. (a suggestion or experiment)

1 Tick (✓) the correct sentences. Correct the sentences with mistakes.

1 He decided buy the house even though it needed to be renovated.
2 I hope to continue to improve my level of spoken English.
3 They promised visiting me in Spain after I moved there.
4 She refused to help him with his homework.
5 She expected not getting the job because the interview hadn't gone well, but the next day she received an offer.
6 The lawyers spent all night working on the case and luckily managed finish just in time.

2 Choose the correct options to complete the sentences.

1 I can't stop **to chat** / **chatting**. I'm in a hurry.
2 I didn't get round **to do** / **to doing** the housework yesterday, so I'll have to do it today instead.
3 The teacher insisted on the students **being** / **be** on time for the school trip.
4 I admit **to lie** / **lying** to my parents about the time the party finished last night.
5 I regret not **accepting** / **accept** the offer of a job in Berlin.
6 Now that I study from home, I miss **talking** / **talk** to my friends at school.
7 If you forget **to go** / **going** to the supermarket, we won't have anything for dinner.

Reported speech

Tenses

When we report what someone else said (direct speech, e.g. *I am cold*), we are usually reporting some time after the actual speech, so we change the tenses used by the original speaker (reported speech, e.g. *He said he was cold*.).

Direct speech	→	Reported speech
present simple	→	past simple
present continuous	→	past continuous
will	→	would
is/am/are going to	→	was/were going to
past simple	→	past perfect
past continuous	→	past perfect continuous
present perfect	→	past perfect
can/may/might	→	could

If the verb in direct speech is past perfect, we don't change it. These verbs don't change either when they are reported: *could, would, might, ought to* and *used to*.

When we report *must*, we usually use *had to*:

'I **must buy** some new trainers.' → She said she **had to buy** some new trainers.

But we use *must* not *had to* when we report a negative or a deduction:

'You mustn't tell Sam.' → She said we **mustn't** tell Sam.
'Giulia must be tired.' → She said that Giulia **must** be tired.

Say and tell

We often use *say* and *tell* to report speech:

He **said** (that) he would be late.
He **said to me** (that) he would be late. (**not** He said me …)
He **told me** (that) he would be late. (**not** He told to me … or He told that …)

Other common reporting verbs are *add, agree, answer, explain, promise* and *reply*. The *to* + infinitive is usually used after them: *He promised/agreed to be quiet*.

Reporting questions

When we report questions, we don't use the question form of the verb and there is no question mark.

Questions with question words (*who, what, how*, etc.) keep the question words when reported:

'How do you feel?' → Peter asked Tom how he felt. (**not** Peter asked Tom how did he feel.)

Questions we can answer with yes or no are reported with *if* or *whether*:

'Do you like my new shoes?' → Rachel asked Tom **if/ whether** he liked her new shoes.

3 Choose the correct option, A or B.

1 He explained that he .... higher than anyone else in his class.
  A could jump   B can jump
2 My sister said that she .... some candles for the cake, if we wanted some.
  A might buy   B may buy
3 He whispered that he .... swim.
  A can't   B couldn't
4 She told them that they .... better in their exams this year.
  A must do   B had to do
5 He stated that he .... to go to the cinema than the theatre.
  A would prefer   B will prefer
6 The teacher told the pupils they .... their calculators in the exam.
  A mustn't use   B had not to use

UNIT 8

Relative clauses

We use *which, who, where* or *whose* to join two ideas about a thing or things.

This is my camera. I had it for my birthday. It has stopped working.
→ *This camera, **which** I had for my birthday, has stopped working.* (**not** which I had it for my birthday – we use *which* instead of *it*)

*The pool **where** we usually swim is closed today.*

- There are two kinds of relative clauses: defining and non-defining.

  Defining relative clauses tell us essential information about the things or people they refer to:

  The girl who won the competition lives next door to me. (If we remove the underlined words, we don't know which girl is being described.)

  The shop where I bought this laptop has a sale. (If we remove the underlined words, we don't know which shop.)

  The boy whose father owns the garage sold me his bicycle. (If we remove the underlined words, we don't know which boy.)

- Non-defining relative clauses tell us extra information about the things or people they refer to:

  My brother, who is three years older than me, won a competition yesterday.

  My bicycle, which I haven't had very long, is too small for me.

  The important information is about the competition / size of the bicycle and the underlined words are extra information – we don't need them.

Defining relative clauses

1 are never separated from the rest of the sentence by commas:
  The bag which I left on the bus was never found.
2 often use *that* instead of *who* or *which*:
  *Who is the girl **that** you were talking to?*
  *There's a new shop in the village **that** sells computer games.*
3 often omit the relative pronoun if it is the object of the verb in the relative clause:
  *The programme about famous scientists (**which**/**that**) I saw last night was really interesting.* (The relative clause begins with a new subject (*I*) so we can omit *which/that*.) We can say:
  The bus that I usually catch to school didn't come today. **or**
  The bus I usually catch to school didn't come today.

  But we keep the relative pronoun if it is the subject of the verb in the relative clause:
  The scientist who was on TV last night works with my dad. (*was* refers back to the scientist so we can't omit *who*.)
  (**not** The scientist was on TV last night works with my dad.)

GRAMMAR REFERENCE 93

Non-defining relative clauses

1 must be separated from the rest of the sentence by commas:
Sam's granny, who lives in Switzerland, used to be a champion skier.
2 never use *that*:
My uncle, who is an actor, often comes to stay.
(**not** *My uncle, that is an actor, often comes to stay.*)
3 never omit the relative pronoun:
*Katya, **whose** family own a restaurant, is coming to the film with us.*
4 sometimes refer to the whole of the main clause:
My cousins in Canada have invited me to spend the summer with them, which is really fantastic! (The idea of spending the summer in Canada is fantastic.)

Prepositions in relative clauses

In informal sentences, we put the preposition at the end:
That's my sister. The teacher is talking to her. →
*That's my sister **who** the teacher is talking **to**.*

Peter had a party. He invited me to it. It was very good. →
*Peter's party, **which** he invited me **to**, was very good.*

If the sentence is very formal, we can put the preposition before the relative pronoun:
*We will address the problem **to which** you refer at the school council meeting.*

1 **Choose the correct relative pronoun.**

1 Ljubljana, **which / where / whose** is the capital of Slovenia, is a city famous for its history and culture.
2 Owen, **who / whose / which** father is from Rio de Janeiro, speaks English and Portuguese fluently.
3 This camera, **who / which / where** I bought on holiday, takes absolutely superb photos.
4 Cambridge University, **which / where / whose** Stephen Hawking studied, is famous for its beautiful old buildings.
5 Mr Barrett, **who / which / where** is my biology teacher, is going to retire in the near future.
6 The film star Ryan Gosling, **which / who / whose** has starred in numerous successful films, was born in Canada.

2 **Complete the sentences with a relative pronoun.**

1 The furniture .... was damaged by yesterday's fire is being repaired.
2 The place .... the car had been abandoned was a pedestrian precinct.
3 The train .... I intended to catch was delayed.
4 The nurse .... I was hoping to see wasn't on duty when I arrived at the medical centre.
5 The man .... spoke at the meeting was very knowledgeable.
6 That's the woman .... cat likes to sleep in my garden.

3 **Rewrite each pair of sentences as one sentence using relative clauses.**

1 The music was by Beethoven. Sandra was playing the music last night.
The music which ....
2 The flute was not hers. Sandra was playing the flute in the concert.
The flute that ....
3 Luke is Sandra's music teacher. Luke lent Sandra a flute.
Luke, ...
4 We've just listened to Sandra's latest recording. Sandra's recording is in the top ten in the classical charts.
We've just listened ....
5 Sandra's mother is very proud of her. Sandra's mother was in the audience tonight.
Sandra's mother, ...
6 Tomorrow, Sandra is going back to London. Sandra goes to music school in London.
Tomorrow, Sandra is ....

4 **Put the words in order to make sentences.**

1 she could / spent / in Toulouse / She / improve / her French. / a semester / so that
2 is taking part in / he can improve / skills. / in order that / his / a training course / He / project management
3 early / rush-hour traffic. / I / the office / the / in order to / left / avoid
4 washed / so as not to / her housemates. / dirty dishes / Martha / all of / annoy / her
5 warm clothes / in order not to / should / in the winter / catch a cold. / You / wear

Irregular verbs

Infinitive	Past simple	Past participle
break	broke	broken
bring	brought	brought
broadcast	broadcast	broadcast
build	built	built
choose	chose	chosen
cost	cost	cost
cut	cut	cut
deal	dealt	dealt
draw	drew	drawn
fly	flew	flown
forget	forgot	forgotten
grow	grew	grown
hear	heard	heard
hit	hit	hit
hold	held	held
mean	meant	meant
pay	paid	paid
rise	rose	risen
shake	shook	shook
sing	sang	sung
sink	sank	sunk
sleep	slept	slept
spend	spent	spent
spill	spilt	spilt
steal	stole	stolen
swear	swore	sworn
teach	taught	taught
wear	wore	worn
win	won	won

Writing bank

WRITING PART 1: ESSAY

1 Read the exam task. What question should you answer? What ideas should you include?

> In your English class you have been talking about the environment. Now, your English teacher has asked you to write an essay.
>
> Write your essay using **all** the notes and giving reasons for your point of view.
>
> *Will environmental problems be worse in 20 years?*
>
> **Notes**
> Write about:
> 1 pollution
> 2 climate change
> 3 your own idea

2 Study the model answer below. What extra idea does it include?

3 Read the essay question. Then decide which ideas would be relevant to include in the essay.

We shouldn't spend so much money on exploring space. Do you agree?

1 It costs a huge amount of money to send rockets into space.
2 Rockets have extremely powerful engines.
3 There are more important problems in the world that we should spend money on.
4 We can learn a lot about our own planet and solar system.
5 People first landed on the moon in 1969.
6 A lot of people in the world don't have food or shelter.
7 I would love to go into space one day.
8 Some important scientific experiments can be carried out in space.

4 Look at the plan for a student's essay on the question in Exercise 3. Decide which paragraph the relevant sentences from Exercise 3 could go in.

> **Introduction**
> [1] .... Is it worth the money?
>
> **Arguments against exploring space**
> [2] ...., ...
>
> **Arguments for exploring space**
> [3] ...., ...
>
> **Conclusion**
> We can learn things from exploring space, but it's probably a luxury the world can't afford.

MODEL ANSWER

[1]In my opinion, [2]it is possible that environmental problems will be worse in 20 years. We already face a large number of serious environmental problems and, if steps are not taken to tackle them, they will become even more serious.

[3]Firstly, there is already a huge amount of pollution in the world, for example from cars, lorries and planes. There is also a big problem with the amount of rubbish that we produce, which often ends up in the sea.

Secondly, [4]our modern way of life produces harmful gases which are causing the planet to become warmer. This is a very serious problem for animals such as polar bears, [5]which may die out if the ice that they live on melts.

Finally, the world's population is growing rapidly and this will put even more pressure on the Earth's resources. More people means more food production, more pollution and more waste.

[6]In conclusion, the world faces some very serious environmental problems which will definitely be worse in 20 years if nothing is done to solve them. [7]However, I am optimistic that scientists and politicians will find ways to improve the situation.

[1]Use phrases to express your own opinion.

[2]Start with a general introduction to the topic.

[3]Use words and phrases to organise your essay and make it clear when you are introducing a new topic.

[4]Give information which is relevant to the topic.

[5]Give reasons to support your arguments and opinions.

[6]End with a clear conclusion.

[7]Use linking words to add similar or contrasting ideas.

5 Read the essay question. Then choose the best introduction and conclusion. Why is it the best one?

Do you think it is better to watch films in the cinema or at home?

1 Introductions

A There are loads of amazing films nowadays. Personally, I love science-fiction films and I often watch them with my friends.

B Watching a film on the big screen at the cinema is certainly very impressive. But in my opinion, there are also advantages to watching films at home with friends.

C Going to the cinema is quite expensive, and some people can't afford it. Also, some small towns don't have a cinema.

2 Conclusions

A To sum up, I hardly ever go to the cinema because there isn't one very close to where I live. But I often watch movies with my friends at the weekend.

B On balance, some people prefer going to the cinema to watch films, and some people prefer to watch films at home. There are lots of different reasons for this. For example, some people can't afford to go to the cinema.

C In conclusion, I would say that for most films, it is more enjoyable to watch at home with a few friends. However, for films with a lot of special effects, it is worth the trip to a cinema to see these on the big screen.

6 Study the words and expressions in the Key language box.

KEY LANGUAGE FOR ESSAYS

Ordering your ideas:
firstly, secondly, finally

Expressing your opinion:
in my opinion, in my view, I would say that, personally, I think

Giving reasons:
because, as, since

Giving results or consequences:
consequently, as a result, therefore, for this reason

Giving examples:
for example, for instance, such as, one example of this is

Linking similar ideas:
in addition to this, furthermore, moreover

Linking contrasting ideas:
however, on the one hand / on the other hand, in contrast, although, whereas

Giving a conclusion:
in conclusion, to sum up, on balance

7 Choose the correct options to complete the sentences.

1 In my opinion, computers are essential in schools **as / for this reason** students need them to find information.
2 It is clearly necessary to test new medicines, but **in my opinion / therefore** this doesn't justify using animals.
3 Cars create a lot of pollution in city centres. **In addition to this / Consequently**, they can cause accidents.
4 There are several reasons why I am against exams. **Finally / Firstly**, they only test what someone can remember on one particular day.
5 Sports **such as / furthermore** tennis and football are more sociable than running.

8 Read the exam task and use the table to plan your essay.

> In your English class you have been talking about city life. Now, your English teacher has asked you to write an essay.
>
> Write an essay using **all** the notes and giving reasons for your point of view.
>
> *Some people believe that cycling is the best way to travel around cities. Do you agree?*
>
> **Notes**
> Write about:
> 1 health
> 2 safety
> 3 your own idea

	Ideas	Useful phrases
Introduction		
Paragraph 1		
Paragraph 2		
Paragraph 3		
Conclusion		

9 Write your essay. Remember to write between 140 and 190 words.

10 Check your essay and make changes if necessary.
- Have you answered the question in the task?
- Have you included the two ideas in the task and added your own idea?
- Have you included only relevant information?
- Have you started with an introduction and ended with a conclusion?
- Have you ordered your ideas into paragraphs?
- Have you given reasons for your ideas and opinions
- Have you used words and phrases to link ideas?
- Have you used between 140 and 190 words?

WRITING BANK

WRITING PART 2: EMAIL / LETTER

1 Read the exam task. Who should you write an email to? What should you write about in your email? What questions should you answer?

> You have received this email from your English-speaking friend, Jo.
>
> > I guess you've been in your new home for about a month now. All your old friends are really keen to know how you're getting on. What's your new home like? And are there lots of exciting things to do in the city? Also, have you made plenty of new friends?
> >
> > Write and tell me all about it!
> >
> > Jo
>
> Write your **email** in 140–190 words.

2 Study the model answer below. Does it answer all the questions in Jo's email? Is the tone formal or informal?

3 Read this task. Then decide if the sentences below are true or false.

> You see this notice in your college.
>
> > Our college wants to organise an event this summer to raise money for schools in developing countries. Below are some of our ideas. Please email me to let me know which you think is the best idea and why. Please also tell us how we should organise the event, to make sure it is a success.
> > 1 a fun sports day   2 a quiz evening   3 a concert
> > Thank you for your help.
> > Anna Bradley, Principal
>
> Write your **email**.

1 You need to write a notice about the event.
2 You have to choose one idea.
3 You should explain your reasons for choosing this.
4 You should suggest a date for the event.
5 Your email is to the college principal.
6 You should use an informal tone.

4 Choose the four sentences that are suitable to include in your email to the principal in Exercise 3. Why are they suitable?

1 I think it's a great idea to raise money for schools in developing countries.
2 I would suggest that a fun sports day would be the best option.
3 I think a quiz evening would be amazing!
4 Loads of people enjoy listening to live music.
5 Concerts are extremely popular with lots of people of different ages.
6 I think it would be a good idea to keep the ticket price fairly low.
7 Why don't you serve food during the event, too?
8 I'm sure that the event will be a huge success and hopefully it will raise a large amount of money.

MODEL ANSWER

¹Hi Jo,

²It was great to hear from you! I miss all my old friends, but I'm getting used to living here in Manchester now.

³My new flat is amazing! It's modern and quite big, and it's got a lovely balcony which looks out over a park. There's also a large living room with comfortable sofas and our new huge TV! My room's quite small, but I don't mind that because I'm out during the day, so I only use it for sleeping.

⁴Manchester's a really lively city. Did you know it's the biggest university city in Britain, so there are loads of young people here. There's always something new and exciting to do. I've discovered some amazing music venues where there are live bands.

⁵I've been lucky with friends and I've met some really nice people here. I'm seeing some of them this evening, to go to the cinema, and I know ⁶you'll get on with them when you meet them. When are you going to come and visit me? Let me know when you're free and we can fix a date.

⁷See you soon,

Ali

¹Use a suitable greeting.
²Give a reason for writing.
³Answer the first question.
⁴Answer the second question.
⁵Answer the third question.
⁶In an informal email/letter, use informal words and phrases.
⁷Use a suitable ending phrase.

5 Choose the correct options in this formal email.

(1) **Dear Ms Copeland,** / **Hi Anne,**

I am writing (2) **because of** / **in response to** your advertisement for staff to work in your hotel this summer. I am (3) **currently** / **at the moment** studying hotel management at college and (4) **would love to work** / **would be interested in working** in your hotel.

I have (5) **learnt all about** / **studied different aspects of** hotel work as part of my course, and I also have some experience of hotel work as I (6) **was employed** / **had a job** in a large international hotel in Spain for six weeks last summer. I worked mainly as a waiter, but also (7) **gained some experience as** / **had a go as** a receptionist when the regular receptionist was ill.

I am friendly and hardworking, and work well as part of a team. I also understand that in a hotel, (8) **keeping the customer happy** / **customer satisfaction** is the most important thing.

(9) **I would be grateful if you would** / **Please will you** consider me for a position in your hotel.

(10) **I look forward to hearing from you.** / **Write soon!**

Joseph Brown

6 Study the words and expressions in the Key language box.

KEY LANGUAGE FOR FORMAL EMAILS AND LETTERS

Opening a formal email/letter:
Dear (Mr/Mrs/Ms Edwards), Dear Sir/Madam,

Giving reasons for writing:
I am writing in response to … I saw your notice/advert in …

Referring to something mentioned in the letter/notice/advert:
Your letter/notice/advert mentioned that … Your letter/notice/advert asked for …

Making suggestions / giving advice:
It would be a good idea to … It might be sensible to … You might like to consider …

Offering to do something:
I would be able/willing to … if necessary.

Making requests:
Would it be possible for you to … ?

Asking for information:
Could you give me some information on … ? Could you let me have more details about … ?

Apologising:
I would like to apologise for …

Closing a formal email:
Yours sincerely (after Dear Mr Edwards), Yours faithfully (after Dear Sir/Madam), I look forward to hearing from you, Kind regards

Tip: Only use Mrs if you are sure that the woman you are writing to is married. Otherwise, use Ms.

7 Correct the mistakes in the sentences from formal and informal letters/emails.
1 It was great hear from you.
2 Why you don't come and visit me in July?
3 I would able to help with the arrangements.
4 I look forward hearing from you.

8 Read the exam task and use the table to plan your letter.

You see this advertisement in your local English-language newspaper.

Staff wanted for summer work
We require staff to work with our English-speaking guests in our busy hotel this summer.
We are looking for people for the following roles:
• Waiter
• Coffee-bar assistant
• Receptionist
Write to Maria Simpson at Top Beach Hotel saying which job interests you and why, and explain why you would be suitable for the job.

Write your **letter** in **140–190** words.

	Ideas	Useful phrases
Writing to?		
Formal or informal?		
Opening phrase		
Point 1		
Point 2		
Point 3		
Ending		

9 Write your letter. Remember to write between 140 and 190 words.

10 Check your letter and make changes if necessary.
- Have you covered all the points in the task?
- Have you used an appropriate formal or informal tone?
- Have you used a range of phrases for giving advice, making suggestions, etc.?
- Have you used a suitable opening and ending?
- Have you used a wide range of language?
- Have you used between 140 and 190 words?

WRITING BANK 99

WRITING PART 2: REVIEW

1 Read the exam task. What should you write a review of? What points should you include? Where will people read your review?

> You see this notice in an English-language magazine.
>
> **Film reviews wanted**
> What films have you seen recently? Write a review of a film you have seen, explaining what it was about and whether you enjoyed it or not. Tell us whether or not you think other people would enjoy it.
>
> The best reviews will be published in next month's magazine.
>
> Write your **review**.

2 Study the model answer below and answer the questions.

1 Does the review cover all the points in the task?
2 Did the writer enjoy the film?
3 Who does the writer think will enjoy the film?
4 Is the language in the review formal and neutral, or informal and friendly?

3 Read the review task. Then look at the two student plans. Which plan is better? Why?

> **Reviews wanted!**
> What shopping websites have you used recently? Write a review of a shopping website that you have used. Say what you bought, how pleased you were with the product, and talk about any problems you experienced. Say whether you would recommend the site to others.

A **Introduction**
Name of website TechWorld, and basic information (what they sell)
What I bought (a new tablet)

My experience
The website – why I like it (easy to use, good prices)
The product – why I was pleased with it (good quality)

A few problems
Slow delivery, missing case, but they dealt with this quickly

Recommendation
Great website for anyone who is looking for a low-priced tablet or other device

B **Introduction**
Why I chose to use this website (looking for a cheap tablet, easier to buy online than go into town)

The website
How I found out about it, how I chose my tablet, problem of slow delivery

Games
Why I like it (I needed a new tablet for playing games)

Conclusion
I'm very pleased with my new tablet and it was very cheap

MODEL ANSWER

¹*Black Panther*
I watched the film *Black Panther* for the first time last week. ²It's a superhero film, in the same genre as *Superman* and *Spiderman*, and has been extremely popular around the world.
³Although I am not usually a big fan of superhero films, ⁴I was really impressed with this one. The story is fairly traditional, with the hero T'Challa (Black Panther) defeating the evil Killmonger, who is trying to gain power over the whole world. ⁵But the action is gripping and the special effects are spectacular. Chadwick Boseman, who plays T'Challa, acts superbly, and really brings the comic-book character to life. The brilliant costumes and music also really help make the film a great spectacle.
³On the negative side, ⁶I felt that there was sometimes a bit too much violence, which makes it unsuitable for young children, and of course you have to accept that the plot is slightly predictable because the good guy will always win.
In spite of this, ⁷I loved the film and ⁸anyone who enjoys fantasy movies will definitely like it.

¹ includes the name of the film as the title
² briefly describes the film in the introduction
³ is organised into clear paragraphs, which focus on positive and negative aspects
⁴ uses a range of phrases to express a personal opinion
⁵ praises positive features and says why the film is good
⁶ includes some negative features, to give a balanced view
⁷ clearly states the writer's opinion in the conclusion
⁸ includes a recommendation, saying who would enjoy the film

4 We often use adjectives or phrases to give our opinion about something in an indirect way. Match the beginnings and endings of the sentences.

1 I was disappointed to
2 We were delighted that
3 I'm absolutely thrilled with
4 The tent isn't as big
5 The food was even better
6 There weren't enough

a my new camera.
b seats around the pool for all the guests.
c find that the screen was cracked.
d than I expected.
e as it looked on the website.
f we had a room with a view of the sea.

5 In a review we often use words to express contrast. Complete the sentences with words from the box.

| although   despite   however   spite   though |

1 The weather was terrible, but in .... of this, we thoroughly enjoyed our stay at the resort.
2 Even .... it was rather expensive, we really enjoyed our time at the museum.
3 I would advise anyone to check out this website, ... the problems that I experienced.
4 .... the service was quick and friendly, the food was a little disappointing.
5 The website stated that the bag was black ...., when it arrived it was grey.

6 Study the words and expressions in the Key language box.

KEY LANGUAGE FOR REVIEWS

Praising something:

It is one of the best … I have ever … , The … was absolutely perfect, The … was even better than I expected, I was pleased/delighted to find that … , It was a nice surprise to find that …

Criticising:

The … was rather disappointing, The advertisement said … , but in fact … , I was a little disappointed to find … , There weren't enough …

Recommending:

Anyone who likes … will really enjoy … , Don't miss the chance/opportunity to … , I'm sure everyone will really enjoy … , If you get the chance to see/buy/try … , you should definitely do it, I would advise anyone to …

Advising someone against something:

I would suggest finding a better … than this, I would strongly advise against eating/reading/watching/buying this … , My advice is to avoid this …

7 Choose the correct options to complete the sentences.

1 This show was even better **than** / **as** I expected.
2 The dessert was rather **disappointed** / **disappointing**.
3 Anyone who enjoys crime novels **will** / **can** love this book.
4 Don't **lose** / **miss** the opportunity to visit this theme park.
5 I would suggest **using** / **to use** a different website.
6 I would strongly **advise** / **suggest** against staying at this campsite.

8 Read the exam task and use the table to plan your review.

> You see this advertisement on a travel website.
>
> **Reviews wanted!**
> What holiday resorts have you been to recently?
> Write a review describing the resort, explaining why you did or didn't enjoy your stay there and saying whether it is good value for money.
> The best reviews will be published on our website.
>
> Write your **review**.

Paragraphs	Ideas	Useful phrases
Description of the resort		
Why I enjoyed / didn't enjoy it		
Good value for money?		
Recommendation		

9 Write your review. Remember to write between 140 and 190 words.

10 Check your review and make changes if necessary.
- Have you covered all the points in the task?
- Have you organised your ideas clearly into paragraphs?
- Have you given your own opinion clearly?
- Have you ended with a recommendation?
- Have you used descriptive adjectives and adverbs to make your writing interesting?
- Have you used a friendly tone?
- Have you used between 140 and 190 words?

WRITING PART 2: ARTICLE

1 Read the exam task. What should you write an article about? What points should you include? Where will people read your article?

> You see this notice in an English-language magazine.
>
> **Articles wanted**
>
> My hobby
>
> Write an article about your hobby. Say what it is, how you started doing it, and why you enjoy it.
>
> The best articles will appear in our magazine next week.
>
> Write your **article**.

2 Study the model answer below and answer the questions.

1 Does the article cover all the points in the task?
2 How many paragraphs does it have?
3 How many direct questions does it ask the reader?
4 Is it written in a formal or an informal style?

3 It is important to choose a title and first sentence which will engage your reader and encourage them to read more. Choose the best title and first sentence for an article about Nelson Mandela. Why is it the best?

A Nelson Mandela
I really admire Nelson Mandela because of everything he achieved in South Africa.

B A peaceful transformation
Can you imagine one person bringing peaceful change to a whole country?

C An important figure in South Africa
Nelson Mandela is a very important figure in the history of South Africa.

4 The first sentence in each paragraph (the topic sentence) gives the topic of the paragraph. Match the topic sentences (a–e) with the paragraphs from an article about a favourite place to visit. There are two topic sentences you don't need.

a The people here are incredibly warm and welcoming.
b This is a lovely, relaxing place.
c I first discovered this place about five years ago.
d One thing I really love is the stunning scenery.
e If you love good food, this is a great place to visit.

1 ………. When you look in one direction, you can see the beautiful beach and the clear blue sea. In the opposite direction, there are lovely views of the mountains, which have snow on their peaks all year round.

2 ………. You can find delicious local cheeses, and plenty of fresh fruit and vegetables. And of course there's fresh fish which the fishing boats bring in each day, and which is perfectly cooked in the restaurants by the beach.

3 ………. They always have time to stop and chat and they seem genuinely keen for you to enjoy your stay. You can always find someone to help if you have any problems, too.

MODEL ANSWER

¹The thrill of the stage

²I'll never forget the first day I stepped onto a real theatre stage. I knew immediately that this was my hobby for life! I'm now a member of my local drama club. We put on two shows every year and have a lot of fun while doing so!

³I first started acting by chance. A friend of mine was interested in joining a drama club, and I agreed to go along with her, to give her a bit of support. ⁴And I loved it from the first day!

First, drama is ⁵incredibly challenging. ⁶Not only do you have to learn what you're going to say, but also understand the character you're playing, their role in the play, and then communicate that to the audience.

⁷Another thing I love about drama is how sociable it is. I've made so many good friends at the drama club, and spending time with them working towards a shared goal is extremely rewarding. And in addition to all of this, ⁸what could beat the thrill of appearing under the lights, in front of a cheering crowd?

¹has an interesting title

²has a first sentence which interests the reader and encourages them to read more

³is organised into clear paragraphs, each with a topic sentence

⁴gives the writer's opinions

⁵uses creative language with strong meanings

⁶gives examples to support the ideas

⁷uses structures to add emphasis

⁸ends with a question or a lively final sentence

5 In an article, it is important to use creative words with strong meanings to make your writing more interesting. Replace the bold words and expressions in the sentences with the creative words with similar meanings from the box.

> absolutely essential   fascinated by
> freezing   huge   packed   terrifying

1 Like a lot of people, I was **interested in** the castle's history.
2 The city centre is always **crowded** with tourists.
3 His first film was a **big** success.
4 I always enjoy watching my local football team play, even when the weather's **cold**.
5 The drive up the narrow mountain road was quite **scary** at times.
6 A good fitness programme is **really necessary** if you're serious about losing weight.

6 You can use structures to emphasise your ideas and opinions in an article. Complete each second sentence so it has a similar meaning to the first sentence but has more emphasis.

1 I admire his determination.
   What ...*I admire is*... his determination.
2 I like the freedom you get when you go hiking.
   The thing .... the freedom you get when you go hiking.
3 Her honesty really surprised me.
   One thing .... her honesty.
4 I will never forget our evening barbecues on the beach.
   What .... our evening barbecues on the beach.
5 I noticed how happy everyone looked.
   The thing .... how happy everyone looked.

7 Study the words and expressions in the Key language box.

KEY LANGUAGE FOR ARTICLES

Catching the reader's attention:
Have you ever … ? I want to tell you about … , It's the best …

Ordering ideas:
first(ly), second(ly), finally

Linking similar ideas:
moreover, in addition to this

Linking contrasting ideas:
while, whereas

Linking results:
therefore, which means

Emphasising ideas:
What I love/admire the most is … , The thing I like best is …

Giving your opinion:
In my opinion … , For me … , As far as I'm concerned …

8 Complete the sentences with one word in each space.
1 .... me, sailing is the best sport in the world!
2 Painting is relaxing, creative and fun, and .... addition to this, you can earn a bit of money by selling your paintings.
3 As far .... I'm concerned, cooking is the best hobby.
4 Hiking isn't expensive, ... means that anyone can do it.
5 I want to .... you about something amazing that happened to me last year.
6 .... I love most is watching live shows in a theatre.

9 Read the exam task and use the table to plan your article.

> You see this notice on an English-language fitness website.
>
> **Articles wanted**
> **Staying healthy**
> How important is your health to you? What do you think are some of the best ways to stay fit and healthy?
> The best articles will appear on our website next month.
>
> Write your **article**.

	Ideas	Useful phrases
How important is health to me?		
Good diet		
Exercise		

10 Write your article. Remember to write between 140 and 190 words.

11 Check your article and make changes if necessary.
- Have you covered all the points in the task?
- Have you organised your ideas clearly into paragraphs?
- Have you got an interesting title and first sentence?
- Have you given your own opinions clearly?
- Have you used creative vocabulary with strong meanings?
- Have you used structures to add emphasis?
- Have you used between 140 and 190 words?

WRITING PART 2: REPORT

1 Read the exam task. Who is the report for? What points should you include?

> A group of English-speaking students wants to visit your city. The group leader has asked you to write a report that includes the following information:
> - the best time of year to visit
> - some interesting places to visit in your city
> - the best way to get around the city
>
> Write your **report**.

2 Study the model answer. Does it cover all the points in the exam task?

3 Read the exam task. Then match the headings with three paragraphs from the report.

> Your English teacher wants to take your class for a meal to celebrate the end of the year, and has asked you to suggest a restaurant in your area. Describe a restaurant that you know and say why it would be popular with your classmates.
>
> 1 The restaurant 2 Advantages of this restaurant 3 Why it would be popular

a
The food is all freshly cooked and the dishes are reasonably priced. There are often daily specials, which are especially good value. In addition to this, there is a separate room at the back of the restaurant which is excellent for large groups.

b
Students will like it because the staff are always welcoming and there is an informal, friendly atmosphere. People in the class have different likes and needs, and there is a good choice of dishes for everyone, including some excellent vegetarian options. Most people will also be unable to resist the delicious desserts.

c
The restaurant is called Dario's and is located on North Street, quite close to the college. It serves a range of Italian food, including pizzas and pasta.

4 Which personal information would it be useful to include in the report in Exercise 3? Why?

A My cousin doesn't usually like Italian food, but he enjoyed his meal there.
B I eat there quite frequently and am always surprised at how low the final bill is.
C I can get there quite easily from my flat because the bus service is excellent.
D I know one of the waiters who works there, and he has confirmed that the food is excellent.

MODEL ANSWER

Introduction
¹The aim of this report is to make recommendations for a group of students who are interested in visiting York.

²The best time of year to visit
York can be cold during the winter, and extremely busy with tourists during the summer. However, the spring is often warm and the city is quiet, so this is a good time to visit. ³For this reason, I usually encourage my friends to visit in April or May.

⁴Places of interest
The city has numerous attractions which reflect its long and fascinating history. ⁵The must-see places are the city walls, the tiny streets in the Shambles area of the old city and the Castle Museum.

Transport
York is a small city, and easy to get around on foot. However, ⁶I would strongly recommend buying a York Pass, which not only includes entry to the top attractions, but also allows travel on the Hop-on, Hop-off tourist bus. It therefore offers a practical and good value transport option.

⁷Conclusion
To sum up, I am sure the students will enjoy seeing the sights in York, and I look forward to welcoming them when they come.

¹Start with a general introduction which gives the aim of the report.

²Use clear headings for the different points.

³Include a small amount of personal information to make the report interesting to read.

⁴Avoid repeating the exact words in the input.

⁵Use a neutral tone for most of the report, and avoid expressing your feelings.

⁶Make recommendations.

⁷End with a conclusion.

5 Choose the best introduction and conclusion for the report in Exercise 3. Why is it the best one?

Introductions

A In this report I'm going to recommend the best Italian restaurant for our class meal.
B This report describes the advantages and disadvantages of a particular restaurant, and discusses whether it would be suitable for a class meal.
C This report aims to give information about a restaurant that I know, and explain why it would be a good choice for a class meal.

Conclusions

A In conclusion, I strongly recommend Dario's because it offers a range of tasty food at good prices and has adequate space to cope with a large group.
B To sum up, Dario's is my favourite restaurant and I'd love to go there with the class.
C On balance, Dario's offers several advantages, especially the desserts, but it also has a few disadvantages.

6 We often use passive forms in reports to make the tone neutral. Complete the passive sentences with the correct words.

1 People often recommend this restaurant for large groups.
This restaurant .... for large groups.
2 People consider this hotel to be one of the best in the area.
This hotel .... one of the best in the area.
3 We expect that around 30 students will attend this event.
It .... that around 30 students will attend this event.
4 People have suggested that a new sports centre should be built.
It .... that a new sports centre should be built.
5 We recommend waterproof clothes for the hiking trip.
Waterproof clothes .... for the hiking trip.

7 Study the words and expressions in the Key language box.

KEY LANGUAGE FOR REPORTS

Introductions:
The aim/purpose of this report is to ... , This report aims to ... , This report looks at ...

Giving advantages and disadvantages:
One advantage is ... , One disadvantage is ... , One problem with this is ...

Linking similar ideas:
in addition to this, furthermore, moreover

Linking contrasting ideas:
however, on the one hand / on the other hand, in contrast, although, whereas

Making recommendations:
I would recommend ... , I strongly recommend ... , I have no hesitation in recommending ...

Giving a conclusion:
in conclusion, to sum up, on balance, all things considered

8 Correct the mistakes in the sentences. Look at punctuation and spelling as well as language mistakes.

1 The aim for this report is to discuss the problems with public transport in Leeds.
2 There are some excellent shops in the shopping centre. In adition to this, there are a number of very good cafés and restaurants.
3 There are very few buses that come to the college moreover the ones that do come are expensive.
4 I have no hesitation in recomending the New Forest for a walking trip.
5 All things consider, the Old Duck would be an excellent choice of hotel.
6 In conclusion I would strongly recommend a new car park in the city centre.

9 Read the exam task and use the table to plan your report.

> The local council wants to improve the shopping centre in your town. Your English teacher has asked students to write a report about the shopping centre, explaining which shops are popular and why, and recommending ways to improve it.

Heading	Ideas	Useful phrases
Introduction		
Paragraph 1		
Paragraph 2		
Paragraph 3		
Conclusion		

10 Write your report. Remember to write between 140 and 190 words.

11 Check your report and make changes if necessary.

- Have you covered all the points in the task?
- Have you organised your ideas under clear headings?
- Have you included only relevant information?
- Have you started with an introduction and ended with a conclusion?
- Have you used words and phrases to link ideas?
- Have you used a formal, neutral tone?
- Have you used between 140 and 190 words?

WRITING PART 2: STORY

1 Read about the story in Part 2 of the Writing paper.

In Part 2 of the Writing paper, you choose a task from three possible ones. One of the tasks might be a story. The task will give you the first sentence of the story, and two ideas that you must include. It will also tell you who the story is for, e.g. a school magazine or an English-language website for young people.

You should make sure you use the first sentence correctly and include the two ideas you are given. You should organise your story into paragraphs, and make sure your story has a clear beginning, middle and end. You should use a range of past tenses, and a range of words and expressions to show when the different events of the story happened. You should write 140–190 words.

2 Read the exam task and answer the questions.

1. What should the first sentence of your story be?
2. What two ideas do you need to include?
3. Where will people read your story?

> You see this notice on an English-language website for young people.
>
> We are looking for stories for our English-language website for young people.
>
> Your story must begin with this sentence:
> *Feeling slightly nervous, Emma walked up the steps and onto the plane.*
>
> Your story must include:
> - bad weather
> - a surprise
>
> Write your **story**.

3 Study the model answer and answer the questions.

1. Does the story start with the first sentence in the task?
2. Does it include the two ideas from the task?
3. Does it have a clear beginning, middle and ending?
4. What past tenses does it use?
5. Does it include descriptions as well as actions?

MODEL ANSWER

¹Feeling slightly nervous, Emma walked up the steps and onto the plane. She ⁴'d never been to America before, but now ²she was on her way for a one-month exchange visit to an American school.

³As she ⁴was waiting for the plane to take off, questions ⁴went through her mind. Would she get on with the other students? Would they accept her? Would it be difficult? Emma sighed. It was too late to change her mind now!

³An hour later, Emma was looking out at the ⁶clear blue sky as they flew over the ocean. Then, ⁵all of a sudden, the sky darkened. There was a roar of thunder and the pilot told passengers to put on their seat belts.

⁵Two minutes later, the plane was in the middle of ⁷a fierce storm. Lightning flashed, and the plane bumped and shook ⁶violently. Terrified, Emma closed her eyes.

After what felt like hours, the plane landed. As she walked out into the terminal building, Emma saw a big colourful sign: Welcome Emma! ⁸What an amazing surprise! Her host family were there, smiling and waving, and Emma knew immediately that ⁹everything would be fine!

¹ starts with the first sentence from the task

² includes some background to the events

³ is organised into paragraphs

⁴ uses past simple, past continuous and past perfect verb forms

⁵ uses a range of time expressions to say when the actions happened and what order they happened in

⁶ uses descriptive adjectives and adverbs to make the story interesting

⁷ includes the idea of bad weather, specified in the task

⁸ includes the idea of a surprise, specified in the task

⁹ includes a clear ending

4 Read the tips.

> Remember, to get a good mark for your story:
> - you must use the first sentence and the two ideas in the input.
> - your story should be organised into paragraphs, and it should have a clear beginning, middle and end.
> - you should use a range of past tenses for the events in the story.
> - you should use a range of words and expressions to show when the different events happened.
> - you should include descriptions as well as actions.
> - you should use descriptive adjectives and adverbs to make your story interesting.
> - you should think of an interesting ending.

5 Read two beginnings of students' stories. Which one is better? Give three reasons why.

> **A** When Laura sat down on the train, she noticed a bag on the seat opposite her. She waved goodbye to her mum, and the train started moving. Laura started reading her book, then the phone in the bag rang.

> **B** When Laura sat down on the train, she noticed a bag on the seat opposite her. There was no one else in her part of the train, so she guessed someone had probably left it there by mistake. It was a very modern, fashionable bag, and looked expensive. Laura opened her book to start reading, when she heard a phone ringing. It wasn't hers – it was coming from inside the bag.

6 Choose the best ending for the story in Exercise 5. Why is it better than the other one?

> **A** Laura stepped down from the train, holding the bag. A woman immediately ran towards her. 'I'm Kirsty,' she said, 'the owner of the bag. Thank you so much for all you did for me today!' Laura handed her the bag. 'No problem,' she said, smiling. 'It certainly made my journey a lot more interesting!'

> **B** When Laura reached her station, she picked up the bag. She wasn't sure what to do with it, so she decided she would take it to the lost property office. Then, all of a sudden, a woman came running onto the train. 'That's my bag!' she said, and grabbed it out of Laura's hands.

7 Study the words and expressions in the Key language box.

> **KEY LANGUAGE FOR STORIES**
>
> **Past simple verbs for the main events:**
> went, found, saw, decided, helped
>
> **Past continuous verbs for longer actions or descriptions:**
> was waiting, were sitting, was raining, was feeling
>
> **Past perfect verbs for earlier actions:**
> had forgotten, hadn't told her, hadn't noticed
>
> **Time expressions:**
> after, as soon as, at first, before, by the time, during, eventually, finally, gradually, in the end, just then, later, meanwhile, suddenly, while, when
>
> **Descriptive adjectives for feelings:**
> determined, enthusiastic, nervous, optimistic, puzzled, relieved
>
> **Descriptive adjectives for the weather:**
> bitter, damp, frosty, mild, misty, stormy
>
> **Descriptive adjectives for places:**
> busy, crowded, peaceful, picturesque, stunning
>
> **Descriptive adverbs:**
> angrily, fiercely, gently, quietly
>
> **Adverbs to comment on what happened:**
> fortunately, luckily, sadly, unfortunately
>
> **Direct speech:**
> 'Hi,' she said. 'Where are you going?' he asked. 'Go away!' she shouted.

8 Add the correct punctuation to the direct speech.
1 Will you come with me he asked.
2 Don't worry he said.
3 Get out she cried.
4 It doesn't matter she said.

9 Read the exam task and plan your story.

> Your teacher has asked you to write a story in English for a school magazine for teenagers.
>
> **Stories wanted**
> We are looking for stories in English for our new school magazine for teenagers.
> Your story must begin with this sentence:
> *When he saw the postman coming up to his door, Matt ran to open it.*
> Your story must include:
> - a mobile phone
> - a new friend
>
> Write your **story**.

10 Write your story in 140–190 words.

Speaking bank

SPEAKING PART 1

1 Read about Part 1 of the Speaking paper.

In Part 1 of the Speaking paper, an examiner asks you personal questions about familiar topics. In Part 1:
- you are with another candidate, but you only speak to the examiner, not the other candidate.
- an examiner asks you questions about yourself, and you answer.
- the questions are about everyday topics such as your family, your hometown, likes and dislikes, your work or studies, free time, travel, celebrations and your future plans.

2 Read the tips.

> To get a good mark in Part 1 of the Speaking paper:
> - you should listen to the questions carefully and make sure you answer the exact questions the examiner asks you.
> - you should use full sentences to answer the questions.
> - you should add reasons, examples or extra information to support your answers.
> - you should express your own opinions.
> - if you don't understand a question, you can ask the examiner to repeat it.
> - you should try to relax and answer the questions in a natural way.

3 Read some typical Part 1 questions. Match each question with a topic (a–e).

1. What do you like about your hometown?
2. What kind of job would you like to do in the future?
3. How do people usually celebrate New Year in your country?
4. When do you usually spend time with your family?
5. What do you normally do at the weekend?
6. Tell us about an enjoyable trip that you went on.
7. Which country would you most like to visit?
8. Which subject did you most enjoy when you were at school?
9. What's the most important festival in your country?
10. What do you enjoy doing in your free time?

a Personal and family life
b Hobbies and free time
c Work and studies
d Travel
e Celebrations

4 🔊 24 Read and listen to Sofia's answers to four of the questions in Exercise 3. Does she add more information to every answer?

MODEL ANSWER

Examiner: What do you like about your hometown?
Sofia: ¹Well, I'm from Milan, in the north of Italy. It's a big city, and I enjoy living there because there's always lots to do, like going to the cinema or music concerts. There are also a lot of young people there, ²so I like that as well.

Examiner: What do you enjoy doing in your free time?
Sofia: Well, I'm quite a sporty person, so I do a lot of exercise. ³For example, I go to the gym two or three times a week, and I play tennis. I also enjoy spending time with my friends.

Examiner: Which country would you most like to visit?
Sofia: I would love to go to Australia. ⁴The reason for this is that I like hot weather and I love going to the beach. The beaches in Australia look amazing. I also think the way of life in Australia is quite relaxed, having barbecues and things like that, so I think I'd enjoy that.

Examiner: Which subject did you most enjoy when you were at school?
Sofia: ⁵Could you repeat that, please?
Examiner: Yes. Which subject did you most enjoy when you were at school?
Sofia: That was definitely geography, because I'm really interested in different countries, and I love learning about how people live in other parts of the world. ⁶I had a very good geography teacher at school too, and I think he made the subject very interesting.

¹Use full sentences in your answer.
²Give your own opinions.
³Add examples to support your answers.
⁴Add reasons to support your opinions.
⁵Ask the examiner to repeat a question if necessary.
⁶Add extra information to make your answer longer.

5 The questions the examiner asks may be about the past, present and future, and it is important to listen carefully and answer correctly. Read six more questions. What do they ask about? Write *past*, *present* or *future*.

1 Tell us about your last holiday or trip. ....
2 How often do you watch TV? ....
3 Which sport would you like to try? ....
4 What things do you usually buy online? ....
5 Which famous person would you most like to meet? ....
6 What kinds of food did you dislike when you were younger? ....

6 Choose the most suitable verb form to complete the answers to the questions in Exercise 5.

1 I .... to Spain last month with some friends.
   A 've been   B would love to go   C went
2 I .... TV very often.
   A don't watch   B didn't watch   C 'm not going to watch
3 I .... skiing because I think it's really good fun.
   A once tried   B 'd like to try   C love
4 I usually .... clothes online.
   A bought some   B buy my   C didn't buy many
5 I .... Ariana Grande because I think she's an amazing singer.
   A 've never met   B meet   C 'd love to meet
6 I .... ice cream!
   A hated   B hate   C 'd hate

7 Write the words and expressions from the box next to the correct function.

| also   as well   because   for example   for instance |
| like   plus   such as   the reason for this is that   too |

1 adding extra information   ....
2 giving a reason   ....
3 giving an example   ....

8 🔊 25 Choose the correct options to complete Dan's answers to three more questions. Listen and check.

Examiner: In what ways do you think you will use English in the future?
Dan: I think I'll use English for my job in the future. **(1) The reason for this is that / Such as** I want to work for an international company, so probably everyone will speak English to each other. I'll probably use it for travelling **(2) too / also**, because I'd like to travel and visit lots of different countries.

Examiner: What do you usually do on your birthday?
Dan: I usually see my family on my birthday **(3) also / because** they like to wish me a happy birthday and they might have presents for me. Then in the evening I usually get together with some friends and do something, **(4) as well / like** go for a meal together.

Examiner: What kind of music do you enjoy listening to?
Dan: I really enjoy R&B music. **(5) For instance, / Too** I like American singers like Rihanna. I'm **(6) as well / also** keen on classical music because I find it very relaxing.

9 Practise answering some of the Part 1 questions in this section. Try to relax and talk about yourself in a natural way.

SPEAKING PART 2

1 Read about Part 2 of the Speaking paper.

In Part 2 of the Speaking paper, you are given a one-minute 'long turn'. In Part 2:
- the examiner will give you two photos on a similar topic and ask you to compare them and answer a question.
- the question you have to answer is written above the photos.
- you speak on your own for around one minute, and no one will interrupt you.
- your partner will talk about a different set of photos.
- when your partner has finished speaking, the examiner will ask you a question about your partner's photos. You will have around 30 seconds to answer this question.

2 Read the tips.

> To get a good mark in Part 2 of the Speaking paper:
> - you should compare the two photos and say what is similar and different about them, rather than just describing them.
> - you should always make it clear which photo you are talking about.
> - you should focus equally on both photos, rather than just talking about one of them.
> - you should speculate about what is happening in the photos and how the people are feeling.
> - you should make sure you allow enough time to answer the question after you have finished comparing the photos.
> - you should listen carefully while your partner is answering, so you can answer the question the examiner will ask you.

3 Read the exam task and look at the photos. What topic connects the two photos? What question do you have to answer?

Examiner: In this part of the test I'm going to give each of you two photographs. I'd like you to talk about your photographs on your own for about a minute, and also to answer a question about your partner's photographs. Tanya, it's your turn first. Here are your photographs. They show people on holiday. I'd like you to compare the photographs and say why you think the people chose these holidays.

SPEAKING BANK

4 🔊 26 Read and listen to the model answer. Does the student say why the people have chosen the holidays?

MODEL ANSWER

¹Both pictures show people on holiday, but they're different kinds of holidays. ²The people in the first photo are in the countryside, ³whereas the second photo shows a big city. ⁴It looks as if the people in the first photo are on a walking holiday, because they've got backpacks and a map. ³On the other hand, the other people are probably doing some sightseeing. They seem to be up in a tower, and they're taking a selfie. Another difference is that the people in the city ⁵look happy and relaxed, whereas the people in the countryside look worried. I think they might be lost. They don't look as happy as the people on the city break. I think the people in the first photo must enjoy walking. ⁶Maybe they chose this holiday because they enjoy being in the countryside. I think the people in the second photo enjoy city life, so ⁶I guess they probably chose to visit this city because there are lots of interesting things to see.

¹Say what is similar about the two photos.

²Make it clear which photo you are talking about.

³Use linking words to compare the photos and say what is different about them.

⁴Speculate about what the people are doing.

⁵Say how you think the people are feeling.

⁶Answer the question when you have finished comparing the photos.

5 🔊 27 Complete the sentences for comparing and contrasting photos with the words from the box. Listen and check.

| as   both   difference   different   other   whereas |

1 ………. pictures show people on holiday.
2 They're ………. kinds of holidays.
3 The people in the first photo are in the countryside, ………. the second photo shows a big city.
4 On the ………. hand, the other people are probably doing some sightseeing.
5 Another ………. is that the people in the city look happy and relaxed.
6 They don't look ………. happy as the people on the city break.

6 🔊 28 Match the beginnings and endings of sentences for speculating about photos. Listen and check.

1 It looks as
2 They're probably doing
3 They seem to
4 They look
5 I
6 They must enjoy
7 Maybe they
8 I guess

a be up in a tower.
b think they might be lost.
c if they're on a walking holiday.
d walking.
e some sightseeing.
f happy and relaxed.
g they probably chose to visit this city because there are lots of interesting things to see.
h chose this holiday because they enjoy being in the countryside.

7 🔊 29 Look at the exam task question and the two photos on page 112. Then listen to three students making mistakes when they complete the task. Match each speaker (1–3) with the mistake that they make (A–D). There is one answer you don't need.

A describes what they can see in both photos, but doesn't compare and contrast them
B focuses too much on one photo
C doesn't give any personal opinions about the photos
D compares and contrasts the photos, but doesn't answer the question

SPEAKING BANK   111

Here are your photographs. They show people preparing food. I'd like you to compare the photographs and say how the people might be feeling about the food they are preparing.
How might the people be feeling about the food they are preparing?

8 🔊 30 Read the task and look at the photos. Complete the task, then listen to the model answer and compare your answers.

Here are your photographs. They show people working. I'd like you to compare the photographs and say what you think might be difficult about the people's jobs.

What might be difficult about the people's jobs?

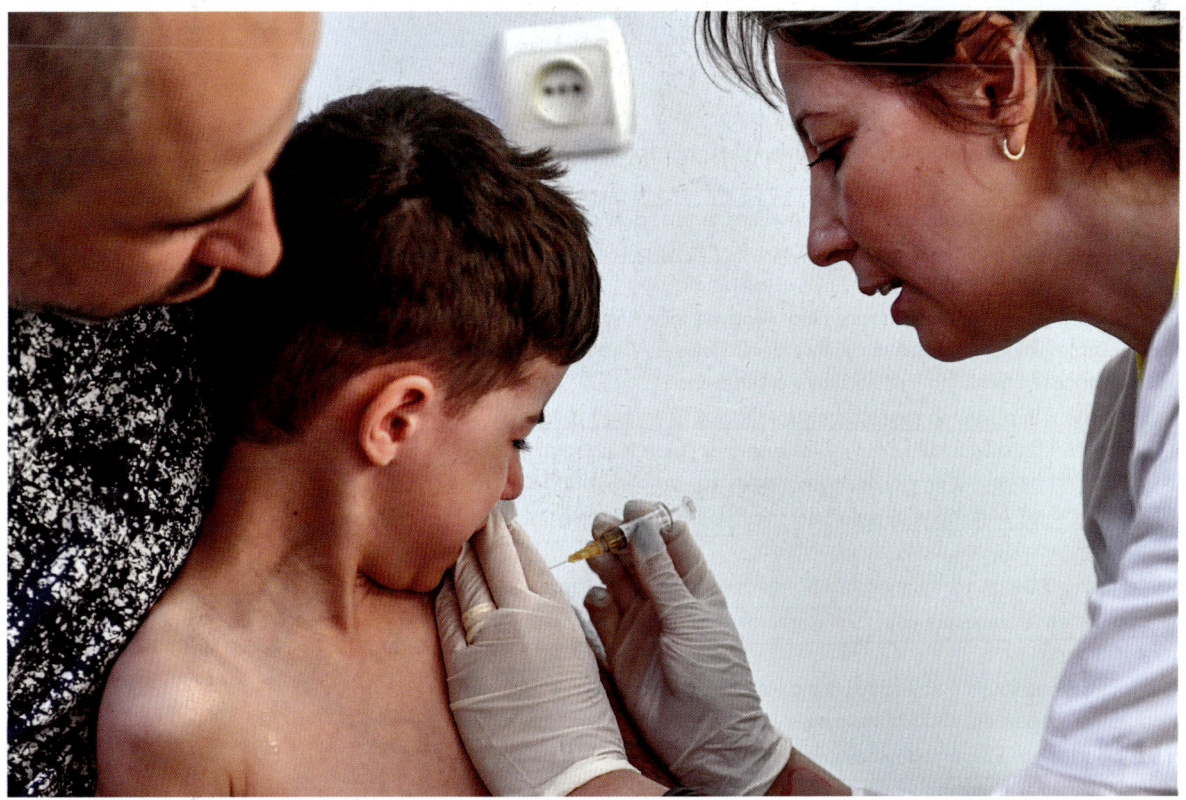

SPEAKING BANK 113

SPEAKING PART 3

1 Read about Part 3 of the Speaking paper.

Part 3 of the Speaking paper lasts for about three minutes, and you work with a partner. In Part 3:

- the examiner will explain an imaginary situation to you, then give you a piece of paper with written prompts that show different ideas or possibilities.
- you must talk with your partner and discuss the prompts, giving your opinions about the different prompts.
- you do not have to discuss all the prompts, but you should discuss most of them.
- there is no right or wrong answer to the task.
- the examiner will then ask you to try to reach agreement about something, and you do this with your partner.
- you do not *have* to reach agreement with your partner, but you should try.

2 Read the tips.

To get a good mark in Part 3 of the Speaking paper:

- you should talk to your partner and listen to your partner – it is important to have a conversation with your partner, rather than just expressing your own ideas.
- you should make suggestions and respond to suggestions that your partner makes.
- you should express your own opinions on the different prompts and respond to your partner's opinions.
- you should give reasons for your opinions.
- you should try to reach agreement with your partner when the examiner asks you to.

3 Read the exam task and read how the examiner will introduce it. What question do you have to discuss? How many prompts are there for you to discuss?

I'd like you to imagine that a hotel wants to attract more guests. Here are some ideas they're thinking about. Talk to each other about why these ideas would attract more guests to the hotel.

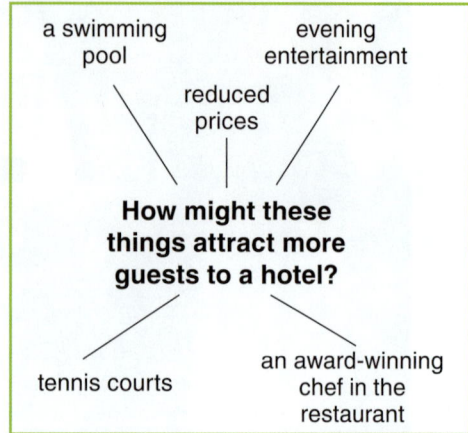

4 🔊 31 Read and listen to Paul and Eva completing the task. How many of the prompts do they discuss? Do they both express their opinions?

MODEL ANSWER

Paul: ¹Shall we start with tennis courts? This sounds like a good idea. A lot of people like playing tennis.

Eva: ²I can see what you mean, but not everyone likes tennis, and a lot of people go on holiday to relax, so they perhaps don't want to do sport. ³I think a swimming pool might be a better idea, because people of all ages can use a swimming pool. Do you agree?

Paul: Yes, you're right. I hadn't thought about that. I agree that a swimming pool's a good idea because people like to sit by it even if they don't swim. ⁴What do you think about the idea of reduced prices? I think that would make a difference.

Eva: ⁵Yes, that's true. There are so many hotels to choose from, and people usually look at the price and try to find a bargain. But I'm not sure that price is enough on its own because people are often happy to pay a bit more money for a hotel with better facilities.

Paul: ⁵Yes, I agree. I think evening entertainment might be a good idea, though. That's a bit different, too, because not many hotels offer it.

Eva: Yes, and it would be good if they offered entertainment for children too, not just adults.

Paul: ⁵Yes, I completely agree with you. ⁴Do you think that having an award-winning chef would attract customers?

Eva: Yes, I do. Everyone loves good food, but a lot of hotels don't have very good restaurants. They could also open the restaurant to everyone, but offer cheaper prices for guests.

Paul: ⁵That's a good idea. I think that would definitely encourage more people to stay at the hotel.

¹Make suggestions to move the discussion to the different prompts.

²Use polite expressions if you disagree with your partner.

³Give your own opinion, and give reasons to support it.

⁴Ask for your partner's opinion.

⁵Use a range of different expressions to agree with your partner.

5 🔊 32 Read the second task that the examiner gives the students, then read and listen to the students completing the task. Do they reach agreement?

Examiner:	Now you have about a minute to decide which idea would be best for the hotel.
Eva:	So, what do you think would be best for the hotel?
Paul:	I'd suggest either the swimming pool or the evening entertainment. Both those things are easy for people to see when they look on the website, and I think they would both be popular with guests.
Eva:	Well, I think everyone enjoys a swimming pool, especially children and young people. But on the other hand, most people only use a swimming pool in the summer, whereas evening entertainment can continue all year, and, like we said, they could offer different entertainment for different ages.
Paul:	That's true, so shall we choose the evening entertainment?
Eva:	Yes, let's go for that.

6 🔊 33 Listen to extracts from three more pairs of students completing the task in Exercise 3. What mistakes do the students make? Match each pair (1–3) with a common mistake (A–D). There is one mistake you don't need.

A The students talk about one prompt for too long, so don't have enough time to talk about the other prompts.
B The students talk for too long individually, don't listen to each other, and don't ask for each other's opinions.
C The students interrupt each other.
D The students talk about things that are not relevant to the task.

7 🔊 34 Match the beginnings and endings of the sentences to make suggestions. Listen and check.

1 It might be a good
2 Perhaps they
3 Tennis courts sound
4 They could
5 I would say that

a like a good idea.
b idea to offer reduced prices.
c offer entertainment for children, too.
d an award-winning chef would be a good idea.
e should have a swimming pool.

8 🔊 35 Choose the correct options to complete the questions you can use to ask your partner's opinion. Listen and check.

1 **Do** / **Are** you agree?
2 What **are** / **do** you think about the idea of a swimming pool?
3 **Will** / **Would** you agree with that?
4 **Do** / **May** you think that's true?

9 🔊 36 Complete the expressions for agreeing and disagreeing with words from the box. Listen and check.

| agree | better | but | mean | right | sure | that's | think |

1 I .... so, too.
2 Yes, ... true.
3 Yes, you're ....
4 I .... with you.
5 I can see what you ...., but I think a swimming pool might be a .... idea.
6 I'm not .... about that.
7 Yes, that's true, ... on the other hand, entertainment would also be popular.

10 🔊 37 Read and listen to the expressions for reaching agreement.
(a) Which two expressions can you use to encourage your partner to reach agreement with you?
(b) Which expression shows that you have reached an agreement?

1 I'd suggest either the swimming pool or the evening entertainment.
2 Are you OK with that?
3 My choice would be the reduced prices.
4 So, shall we choose the evening entertainment?
5 Yes, let's go for that.

11 🔊 38 Read an exam task and practise answering it with a partner. Listen and compare your ideas.

I'd like you to imagine that some people are discussing modern technology. Here are things that some people say it would be difficult to live without. Talk to each other about why it would be difficult to live without these things.

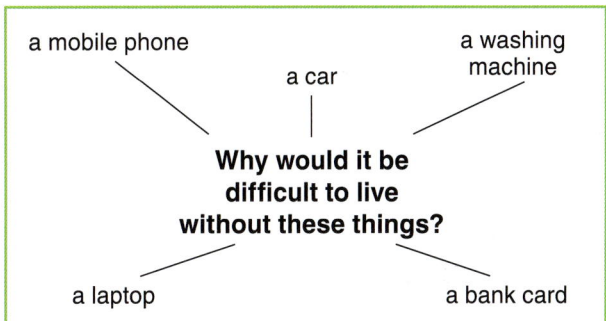

12 🔊 39 Read the second part of the exam task and practise answering it with a partner. Listen and compare your ideas.

Now you have about a minute to decide which thing people would find it the most difficult to live without.

SPEAKING PART 4

1 Read about Part 4 of the Speaking paper.

Part 4 of the Speaking paper lasts for about four minutes, and you work with a partner. In Part 4:

- the examiner will ask you questions on the general topic that you have talked about in Part 3.
- the questions ask you to express your opinion rather than give information.
- the examiner will ask you questions individually, but they may also bring your partner into the discussion after you have answered a question.
- the examiner may also ask you to reply to your partner's opinions.

2 Read the tips.

> To get a good mark in Part 4 of the Speaking paper:
> - you should express your opinions, and give reasons and examples to support your opinions.
> - you should avoid giving short answers, and should always give more information to expand your answers.
> - you should listen carefully when your partner is speaking, so that you can give your opinion on what they have said if you are asked.

3 Read some typical Part 4 questions on the topic of travel and holidays. Do all the questions ask about opinions?

- What is the advantage of going on holiday with friends, rather than with family?
- Some people say that tourism is bad for an area. What do you think?
- What places are popular for holidays in your country?
- Some people say travel is bad for the environment. Do you agree?
- What do you think young people can learn by going travelling?

4 🔊 40 Read and listen to Alex and Nicola discussing two of the questions in Exercise 3. Choose the sentence which describes how they answer.

A They each give their own opinions, but don't listen to each other.
B They listen to each other and respond to what the other says.

MODEL ANSWER

Examiner: Alex, some people say that travel is bad for the environment. Do you agree?

Alex: Yes, I do because ¹I think that when people travel they use fuel, for example in a plane or a car, and that's very bad for the environment. ²They also create a lot of rubbish, for example if they have a picnic on the beach, and that's bad for the environment too.

Examiner: What do you think, Nicola?

Nicola: Well, I agree with Alex that travel can be bad for the environment, but on the other hand, I'd say that you *can* be a responsible tourist. ³For example, I prefer to travel by train because it's better for the environment, and I never leave rubbish. So I think it's possible to travel in a way that isn't bad for the environment.

Examiner: OK. Alex, what do you think young people can learn by going travelling?

Alex: Oh, I think they can learn a lot. For example, they can learn about other cultures and ways of life, and they can also see some of the problems that exist in other parts of the world. I think that travelling is very good for young people.

Examiner: What do you think about this, Nicola?

Nicola: ⁴I completely agree with Alex, and I also think that young people can benefit personally by becoming more independent when they go travelling. For example, when you're travelling you might have to deal with some difficult situations, and if you do this successfully, it can give you a lot of confidence.

¹Make suggestions to move the discussion to the different prompts.

²Give reasons and examples to support your opinions.

³Talk about your own likes, dislikes and preferences.

⁴Agree and disagree with your partner, and respond to what they say.

5 🔊 **41** Listen to three more pairs of students answering Part 4 questions. What mistakes do the students make? Match each pair (1–3) with a common mistake (A–D). There is one mistake you don't need.

A The students' answers are too short, and they don't add more information.
B The students don't listen to each other, so they can't respond to what the other says.
C The students talk about things that are not relevant to the task.
D The students interrupt each other.

6 🔊 **42** Read the tip. Then listen to three students answering Part 4 questions on the topic of food. What extra question does each student have in their mind?

> Sometimes it can be difficult to think of things to say in answer to a Part 4 question. To help, it can be useful to keep question words in your mind: *Why? How? When? Where?* Asking yourself these questions can help you think of extra things to say.

7 Sometimes the examiner might ask you a question that you haven't thought about before. Look at the model answers and notice the strategies that the students use.

MODEL ANSWERS

1
Examiner: Do you think online shopping will ever replace going to shops?
Student: ¹Hmm, let me think. That's an interesting question. I'm not sure that online shopping will ever replace going to the shops because there are some things that people like to see or try before they buy them.

2
Examiner: Do you think that some people spend too much time shopping?
Student: ²Well, it's true that some people spend quite a lot of time shopping. I guess for some people shopping is almost like a hobby. But I think that if they've got plenty of money to spend, then it isn't a problem for them to spend a lot of time in the shops. But I think it's a problem for people who don't have much money, because they might spend too much if they spend a lot of time shopping.

3
Examiner: Is it better to go shopping alone or with friends?
Student: ³I think that there are some advantages to shopping alone, for example, you can find things more quickly and you probably don't spend as much money. On the other hand, shopping with friends is more fun because you can chat about things and go for a coffee together. So I think I would probably say that shopping with friends is better for this reason.

¹Use expressions to give yourself time to think about your ideas, then give your opinion.

²Start with a general statement about the topic of the question, then develop the idea and give your opinion.

³Give one point of view and then the opposite point of view, then give your own opinion.

8 🔊 **43** Listen to three students answering Part 4 questions about health and fitness. Match each student with the strategy (1–3) from Exercise 7 that they use.

9 🔊 **44** Practise answering these Part 4 questions. Listen and compare your answers.

1 Some people say that there will be no shops in 20 years because people will buy everything online. Do you agree?
2 Are there advantages to living in the countryside rather than a big city?
3 Why do you think that so many people dream of becoming a celebrity?
4 How do you think people benefit from going on holiday?

Phrasal verb builder

Phrasal verbs consist of a verb with a preposition or adverb or both. The meaning of the phrasal verb is different from the meaning of its separate parts. The following are all phrasal verbs.

Phrasal verb	Definition
be into sth	be interested in something
book sb into	reserve a place for somebody at a hotel/event
break up	finish school/college at the end of the term/year
bring up	introduce (a topic in a discussion)
burst out	suddenly start doing something (laughing/crying)
calm sb down	stop somebody feeling angry, upset or excited
check in	arrive and register at a hotel or airport
check out	leave a hotel after paying and returning your room key
cheer up	become happy
copy out	write a written text again on a piece of paper
devote sth to sb	use time, energy, etc. for a particular purpose
drop out	fail to complete something (a university course / a race)
fall behind	not make progress
get away	leave or escape from a person or place
get back	return
get on	board a plane/train/ferry/bus
get through	complete successfully
go away	go on holiday
go over	examine or look at something in a careful or detailed way
hand in	give something (homework) to a teacher
hand out	give something (worksheet) to each of a number of people
keep up with	progress or travel at the same rate/speed as others
listen up	pay attention
look through	quickly read
make up	invent

Phrasal verb	Definition
pick out	identify (details)
point out	direct someone's attention to someone or something
pull out	drive from the side of the road onto a different part of the road
pull over	drive to the side of the road and stop
pull up	stop in a vehicle
read out	read words aloud so that other people can hear
read up	spend time reading in order to find out information about something
refer to	talk or write about somebody or something, especially briefly
rub out	erase
run into sb	meet someone you know when you are not expecting to
run into sth	crash into something (in a vehicle or on a bike)
set out	start a journey
shut up	stop talking or making a noise, or to make somebody stop doing this
speak up	speak loudly and distinctly or to express an opinion freely
stand for	mean
stand up for	defend
stay over	sleep overnight (often at someone's house)
stop over	stay somewhere for one night or more when you are travelling to somewhere else
take off	leave the ground and fly (of an aircraft)
take up	become interested or engaged in a pursuit
talk sb into sth	persuade someone to do something
talk sth over	discuss a problem or situation with someone, often to find out their opinion or to get advice before making a decision about it
tell sb off	express disapproval to someone for doing something bad
turn up	arrive or appear somewhere, usually unexpectedly

Wordlist

adj = adjective, *adv* = adverb, *conj* = conjunction, *n* = noun, *v* = verb, *pv* = phrasal verb, *prep* = preposition, *exp* = expression

UNIT 1

anxiety *n* an uncomfortable feeling of nervousness or worry about something that is happening or might happen in the future

approach *n* a way of doing something

at least *exp* as much as, or more than, a number or amount

at once *exp* immediately

celebrate *v* to have a party or a nice meal because it is a special day or something good has happened

community *n* the people living in a particular area

consequence *n* a result of a particular action or situation, often one that is bad or not convenient

contribute *v* to give something, especially money, in order to provide or achieve something together with other people

demanding *adj* needing a lot of your time, attention or effort

distinguish *v* to notice or understand the difference between two things, or to make one person or thing seem different from another

energetic *adj* having or needing a lot of energy

enhance *v* to improve the quality, amount or strength of something

expose *v* to remove what is covering something so that it can be seen

formal *adj* not casual, official

function *n* the natural purpose (of something) or the duty (of a person)

get away with *pv* to succeed in avoiding punishment for something

highlight *v* to attract attention to or emphasise something important

informal *adj* suitable for when you are with friends or family, but not for official occasions

involved *adj* not simple and therefore difficult to understand

make a comparison *exp* to compare two or more things

nature *n* all the animals, plants, rocks, etc. in the world and all the features, forces and processes that happen or exist independently of people, such as the weather, the sea, mountains, animals or plants

obsession *n* something or someone that you think about all the time

participate *v* to take part in or become involved in an activity

relieved *adj* feeling happy because something bad did not happen

rely *v* to need someone or something in order to be successful

significant *adj* important

support *v* to agree with and give encouragement to someone or something because you want him, her or it to succeed

thrilling *adj* very exciting

tradition *n* a custom or way of behaving that has continued for a long time in a group of people

UNIT 2

activity *n* the situation in which a lot of things are happening or people are moving around

adventurous *adj* liking to try new or difficult things

appeal *n* a request to the public for money, information or help

appearances *n* what things look like or seem to be rather than what they actually are

aware *adj* knowing about something

competition *n* a situation in which someone is trying to win something or be more successful than someone else

confidence *n* when you are certain of your ability to do things well

demand *v* to ask for something forcefully, in a way that shows that you do not expect to be refused

determination *n* the ability to continue trying to do something, although it is very difficult

explorer *n* someone who travels to places where no one has ever been in order to find out what is there

freedom *n* the condition or right of being able or allowed to do, say, think, etc. whatever you want to, without being controlled or limited

identify *v* to recognise someone or something and say or prove who or what that person or thing is

initially *adv* at the beginning

inspiring *adj* encouraging, or making you feel you want to do something

interact *v* to communicate with or react to

investigate *v* to examine a crime, problem, statement, etc. carefully, especially to discover the truth

magical *adj* produced by or using magic

majority *n* the larger number or part of something

motivation *n* enthusiasm for doing something

population *n* all the people living in a particular country, area or place

process *n* a series of actions that you take in order to achieve a result

protection *n* the act of protecting, or state of being protected

rapid *adj* happening or moving very quickly

remote *adj* far away in the distance

revise *v* to look at or consider again an idea, piece of writing, etc. in order to correct or improve it

rural *adj* relating to the countryside and not to towns

unique *adj* being the only existing one of its type or, more generally, unusual, or special in some way

warning *n* something that tells or shows you that something bad may happen

UNIT 3

active *adj* busy with a particular activity

appeal *v* to attract or interest someone

aspect *n* one part of a situation, problem, subject, etc.

be supposed to (do something) *v* to have to; should (do something)

budget *n* the amount of money you have available to spend

cast *n* all the actors in a film or play

character *n* a person in a book, film, etc.

conductor *n* someone who directs the performance of musicians or a piece of music

costume *n* a set of clothes worn in order to look like someone or something else

creativity *n* the ability to produce or use original and unusual ideas

criticise *v* to express disapproval of someone or something

direction *n* the control of a film, play, etc.

emotion *n* a strong feeling such as love or anger

exceptional *adj* very good and better than most other people or things

have trouble (doing something) *exp* to experience difficulties in doing something

hero *n* the main character in a book or film

justice *n* treatment of people that is fair

lyrics *n* the words of a song

opportunity *n* an occasion or situation that makes it possible to do something that you want to do or have to do, or the possibility of doing something

outstanding *adj* excellent and much better than most

overall *adv* in general rather than in particular

passive *adj* not acting to influence or change a situation; allowing other people to be in control

plot *n* the things that happen in a story

producer *n* someone who controls how a film, play, programme or musical recording is made

professional *adj* relating to work that needs special training or education

representative *n* someone who speaks or does something officially for another person or group of people

review *n* a piece of writing in a newspaper that gives an opinion about a new book, film, etc.

rhythm *n* a strong pattern of sounds, words or musical notes that is used in music, poetry and dancing

self-confidence *n* the belief that you can do things well and that other people respect you

set *n* the place where a film or play is performed or recorded, and the pictures, furniture, etc. that are used

shot *n* a short piece in a film in which there is a single action or a short series of actions

soundtrack *n* the sounds, especially the music, of a film, or a separate recording of this

special effects *n* an unusual type of action in a film, or an entertainment on stage, created by using special equipment

stunt *n* when someone does something dangerous that needs great skill, usually in a film

UNIT 4

addiction *n* an inability to stop doing or using something, especially something harmful

analysis *n* the act of analysing something

calculation *n* the process of using information you already have and adding, taking away, multiplying or dividing numbers to judge the number or amount of something

concentration *n* the ability to think carefully about something you are doing and nothing else

consumer *n* a person who buys goods or services for their own use

convenience *n* when something is easy to use and suitable for what you want to do

creation *n* the act of creating something, or the thing that is created

defender *n* someone in a sports team who tries to prevent the other team from scoring points, goals, etc.

disability *n* an illness, injury or condition that makes it difficult for someone to do the things that other people do

expectation *n* the feeling that good things are going to happen in the future

friendliness *n* the quality of behaving in a pleasant, kind way towards someone

genuine *adj* if something is genuine, it is real and exactly what it appears to be

get involved in *exp* to take part in something

infection *n* a condition in which bacteria or viruses that cause disease have entered the body

injury *n* physical harm or damage to someone's body caused by an accident or an attack

inspiration *n* someone or something that gives you ideas for doing something

manufacturer *n* a company that produces goods in large numbers

offence *n* an illegal act; a crime

opponent *n* someone who you compete against in a game or competition

passionate *adj* having very strong feelings or emotions

pitch *n* an area of ground where a sport is played

potential *adj* a potential problem, employer, partner, etc. may become one in the future, although they are not one now

professional *n* someone is a professional if they get money for a sport or activity which most people do as a hobby

recovery *n* the process of becoming well again after an illness or injury

referee *n* someone who makes sure that players follow the rules during a sports game

researcher *n* someone who studies a subject, especially in order to discover new information or reach a new understanding

responsible (for) *adj* having control and authority over something or someone, and the duty of taking care of it or them

tackle *n* the act of trying to get the ball from someone in a game like football

track *n* a path, often circular, used for races

treatment *n* the way you deal with or behave towards someone or something

umpire *n* someone whose job is to watch a sports game and make sure that the players obey the rules

UNIT 5

acquire *v* to get or buy something

adapt *v* to change for a new situation

ambition *n* a strong wish to achieve something

appreciate *v* to feel grateful for something

capacity *n* the total amount that can be contained or produced

come across *pv* to find or meet by chance

come up with *pv* to suggest or think of an idea or plan

community *n* the people living in one particular area, or people who are considered as a unit because of their common interests, social group, or nationality

construction *n* the work of building houses, offices, bridges, etc.

courage *n* the ability to control your fear in a dangerous or difficult situation

eagerness *n* the state of wanting to do or have something very much, especially something interesting or enjoyable

enable *v* to make someone able to do something, or to make something possible

enthusiastic *adj* keen, eager, showing enthusiasm

extent *n* the size or importance of something

facilities *n* buildings or equipment that are provided for a particular purpose

functional *adj* designed to be practical and useful rather than attractive

give up *pv* to stop doing a particular activity or job

go through *pv* to experience a difficult or unpleasant situation

interactive *adj* an interactive system or computer program is designed to involve the user in the exchange of information

look down on *pv* to think that someone is less important than you

participate *v* to take part in or become involved in an activity

politeness *n* behaviour that is socially correct and shows understanding of and care for other people's feelings

profession *n* any type of work that needs special training or a particular skill, often one that is respected because it involves a high level of education

revise *v* to look at or consider again an idea, piece of writing, etc. in order to correct or improve it

set *n* a group of pupils at school who have a similar level in a particular subject

volunteer *n* someone who works without being paid, especially work that involves helping people

wisdom *n* the ability to use your knowledge and experience to make good decisions and judgments

UNIT 6

amateur *n* someone who takes part in an activity for pleasure, not as a job

(the) atmosphere *n* the mixture of gases around the Earth

characteristics *n* a typical or noticeable quality of someone or something

citizen *n* a person who is a member of a particular country and who has rights because of being born there or because of being given rights, or a person who lives in a particular town or city

climate change *n* the way the Earth's weather is changing

coastal *adj* positioned on, or relating to the coast

conservation *n* the protection of plants and animals, natural areas, and interesting and important structures and buildings, especially from the damaging effects of human activity

construct *v* to build something or put together different parts to form something whole

data *n* information, especially facts or numbers, collected to be examined and considered and used to help decision-making, or information in an electronic form that can be stored and used by a computer

endangered *adj* in danger of being harmed, lost, unsuccessful, etc.

environment *n* the air, water and land in or on which people, animals and plants live

extinct *adj* not now existing

fuel *n* a substance that is burnt to give heat or power

habitat *n* the natural environment in which an animal or plant usually lives

interpret *v* to decide what the intended meaning of something is

organic *adj* not using artificial chemicals in the growing of plants and animals for food and other products

pollution *n* damage caused to water, air, etc. by bad substances or waste

pressure *n* difficult situations that make you feel worried or unhappy

recycle *v* to use paper, glass, plastic, etc. again and not throw it away

researcher *n* someone who studies a subject, especially in order to discover new information or reach a new understanding

rubbish *n* things that you throw away because you do not want them

specialist *n* someone who has a lot of experience, knowledge or skill in a particular subject

species *n* a set of animals or plants in which the members have similar characteristics to each other and can breed with each other

transport *n* when people or things are moved from one place to another

urban *adj* of or in a city or town

UNIT 7

admire *v* to like or respect someone or something because they are good or clever

amused *adj* showing that you think something is funny

ashamed *adj* feeling bad because you have done something wrong

aspect *n* one part of a situation, problem, subject, etc.

astonished *adj* very surprised

bargain *n* something on sale at a lower price than its true value

competitive *adj* involving competition

concerned *adj* worried

confused *adj* unable to think clearly or to understand something

critical *adj* saying that someone or something is bad or wrong

designer *adj* made by a famous or fashionable designer

express *v* to show a feeling, opinion or fact

furious *adj* extremely angry

identify *v* to recognise someone or something and say or prove who or what that person or thing is

income *n* money that is earnt from doing work, or received from investments

inspired *adj* excellent, or resulting from inspiration

irritated *adj* annoyed

luxury *n* something that gives you a lot of pleasure but cannot be done often

on the other hand *exp* (usually following *on the one hand*) used to compare two different facts or opinions on a situation

opinion *n* a thought or belief about something or someone

passionate *adj* showing a strong feeling about a subject

profit *n* money that is earnt in trade or business after paying the costs of producing and selling goods and services

purchase *v* to buy something

retail *n* the activity of selling goods to the public, usually in shops

second-hand *adj* if something is second-hand, someone else had it or used it before you

supplier *n* a company, person, etc. that provides things that people want or need, especially over a long period of time

unaffordable *adj* too expensive for people to be able to buy or pay for

vintage *adj* having all the best or most typical qualities of something, especially from the past

whereas *conj* compared with the fact that

UNIT 8

accessible *adj* easy to understand, find or reach

acid *n* any of various usually liquid substances that can react with and sometimes dissolve other materials

aluminium *n* a chemical element that is a light, silver-coloured metal, used especially for making cooking equipment and aircraft parts

atom *n* the smallest unit that an element can be divided into

attachment *n* a computer file which is sent together with an email message

bookmark *n* an address on the internet that you record so that you can quickly find something again

cell *n* the smallest living part of an animal or a plant

combine *v* to (cause to) exist together, or join together to make a single thing or group

conservation *n* the protection of nature

ecology *n* the relationships between the air, land, water, animals, plants, etc., usually of a particular area, or the scientific study of this

electronics *n* the scientific study of electric current and the technology that uses it

element *n* a part of something

endangered *adj* in danger of being harmed, lost, unsuccessful, etc.

evaluate *v* to judge or calculate the quality, importance, amount or value of something

genetics *n* the study of how, in all living things, the characteristics and qualities of parents are given to their children by their genes

geology *n* the study of the rocks and similar substances that make up the Earth's surface

habitat *n* the natural environment in which an animal or plant usually lives

hard drive *n* the part inside a computer that is not removed and stores very large amounts of information

identify *v* to recognise a problem, need, fact, etc. and to show that it exists

inventor *n* someone who has invented something or whose job is to invent things

investigate *v* to try to get all the facts about something

legally *adv* as stated by the law

opinion *n* the thoughts or beliefs that a group of people have

opposite *adj* completely different

origin *n* the beginning or cause of something

oxygen *n* a chemical element that is a gas with no smell or colour. Oxygen forms a large part of the air on Earth, and is needed by animals and plants to live

pollution *n* damage caused to water, air, etc. by harmful substances or waste

probability *n* the level of possibility of something happening or being true

psychology *n* the scientific study of the way the human mind works and how it influences behaviour, or the influence of a particular person's character on their behaviour

reliable *adj* someone or something that is reliable can be trusted or believed because he, she or it works or behaves well in the way you expect

reveal *v* to tell or show someone a piece of (secret) information

species *n* a set of animals or plants in which the members have similar characteristics to each other and can breed with each other

substance *n* a solid, gas or liquid

technology *n* (the study and knowledge of) the practical, especially industrial, use of scientific discoveries

telecommunications *n* the sending and receiving of messages over distance, especially by phone, radio and television

valuable *adj* valuable information, advice, etc. is very helpful or important

Exam information

Part/Timing	Content	Exam focus
Reading and Use of English 1 hour 15 minutes	**Part 1** A modified cloze text containing eight gaps and followed by eight multiple-choice items. **Part 2** A modified open cloze text containing eight gaps. **Part 3** A text containing eight gaps. Each gap corresponds to a word. The stems of the missing words are given beside the text and must be changed to form the missing word. **Part 4** Six separate questions, each with a lead-in sentence and a gapped second sentence to be completed in two to five words, one of which is given as a 'key word'. **Part 5** A text followed by six multiple-choice questions. **Part 6** A text from which six sentences have been removed and placed in a jumbled order after the text. A seventh sentence, which does not need to be used, is also included. **Part 7** A text, or several short texts, preceded by ten multiple-matching questions.	Candidates are expected to demonstrate the ability to apply their knowledge of the language system by completing the first four tasks; candidates are also expected to show understanding of specific information, text organisation features, tone, and text structure.
Writing 1 hour 20 minutes	**Part 1** One compulsory essay question presented through a rubric and short notes. **Part 2** Candidates choose one task from a choice of three task types. The tasks are situationally based and presented through a rubric and possibly a short input text. The task types are: • an essay • an article • a letter or email • a review • a report • a story	Candidates are expected to be able to write using different degrees of formality and different functions: advising, comparing, describing, explaining, expressing opinions, justifying, persuading, recommending and suggesting.
Listening Approximately 40 minutes	**Part 1** A series of eight short unrelated extracts from monologues or exchanges between interacting speakers. There is one three-option multiple-choice question per extract. **Part 2** A short talk or lecture on a topic, with a sentence-completion task which has ten items. **Part 3** Five short related monologues, with five multiple-matching questions. **Part 4** An interview or conversation, with seven multiple-choice questions.	Candidates are expected to be able to show understanding of agreement, attitude, detail, function, genre, gist, main idea, opinion, place, purpose, relationship, situation, specific information, topic, etc.
Speaking 14 minutes	**Part 1** A conversation between the examiner (the 'interlocutor') and each candidate (spoken questions). **Part 2** An individual 'long turn' for each candidate, with a brief response from the second candidate (visual and written stimuli, with spoken instructions). **Part 3** A discussion question with five written prompts. **Part 4** A discussion on topics related to Part 3 (spoken questions).	Candidates are expected to be able to respond to questions and to interact in conversational English.

Acknowledgements

The authors and publishers would like to thank the following contributors:

Grammar on the move: Lucy Passmore and Jishan Uddin

Grammar reference: Laura Matthews, Barbara Thomas and Bryan Goodman-Stephens

Writing and Speaking Bank: Sheila Dignen

The authors and publishers acknowledge the following sources of copyright material and are grateful for the permissions granted. While every effort has been made, it has not always been possible to identify the sources of all the material used, or to trace all copyright holders. If any omissions are brought to our notice, we will be happy to include the appropriate acknowledgements on reprinting and in the next update to the digital edition, as applicable.

Key: U = Unit, Rev = Revision, GrR = Grammar reference, SpB = Speaking bank.

Text

U1: Shortlist Media Limited for the adapted text from 'Friendship anxiety: "Am I the only one who worries they don't have 'enough' friends?"' by Lauren Geall. Copyright © 2010–2022 Stylist. Reproduced with permission of the Shortlist Media Limited through PLSclear; **U2:** The Guardian for the text adapted from 'I took a deep breath': the 10-year-old girl who conquered Yosemite's El Capitan" by Matthew Cantor, The Guardian, 22.06.2019. Copyright © 2021 Guardian News & Media Limited. Reproduced with permission; The Independent for the text adapted from 'Teen Spirit: What's it really like to be a teenager?' by Charlotte Philby, The Independent, 17.07.2012. Copyright © 2012 Independent Digital News & Media Ltd. Reproduced with permission; **U3:** MusicianWave for the adapted text from 'Music Managers – Everything You Need to Know' by Brian Clark, 04.01.2020, available https://www.musicianwave.com. Copyright © 2022 MusicianWave.com. Reproduced with kind permission; **U4:** Furia for the text adapted from pages 9, 10, 11 'The bus arrived…" to "…leave everything we had on the pitch.' by Yamile Saied Méndez, 15.09.2020. Copyright © 2020 by Yamile Saied Méndez. Reprinted by permission of Algonquin Young Readers. All rights reserved; Sky Brown for the text on 'Sky Brown, skateboarder'. Reproduced with permission of Sky & Ocean Productions, Inc. represented by J. McIlwee & Associates; **U8:** Riya Karumanchi for the text on 'Young inventors'; Neil Deshmukh for the text on 'Young inventors'. Reproduced with kind permission; Xóchitl Guadalupe Cruz López or the text on 'Young inventors', available https://blurredbylines.com/articles/xochitl-guadalupe-cruz-lopez-child-inventor-chiapas-mx/. Represented by Blurred Bylines. Reproduced with kind permission; Fionn Ferreira for the text on 'Young inventors'. Reproduced with kind permission.

Photography

The following photographs are sourced from Getty Images:

U1: Gary Hershorn/Corbis News; Puay Ng/EyeEm; Michael Dunning/The Image Bank; SDI Productions/E+; SolStock/E+; Jasmin Merdan/Moment; Westend61; kali9/E+; Maskot; Flashpop/DigitalVision; **U2:** Don Mason/Tetra images; Alex Hibbert/The Image Bank; AscentXmedia/E+; Devon Wohlfahrt/500px; Justin Lambert/DigitalVision; vitranc/E+; saravutvanset/RooM; powerofforever/E+; **U3:** Cimmerian/E+; Joey Foley/FilmMagic; Hill Street Studios/DigitalVision; SolStock/E+; Billy Hustace/The Image Bank Unreleased; visionchina/E+; Peter Muller/Image Source; monzenmachi/iStock/Getty Images Plus; monkeybusinessimages/iStock/Getty Images Plus; shironosov/iStock/Getty Images Plus; andresr/E+; Tom Wilde/Stone; **U4:** Guenther Iby/Getty Images Sport; Ian Hitchcock/Getty Images Sport; vitranc/E+; Jean Catuffe/Getty Images Sport; FatCamera/E+; LJM Photo/Design Pics; Trevor Williams/DigitalVision; Oscar Wong/Moment; Ron Levine/Stone; Camille Tokerud/Stone; Astrakan Images/Image Source; **U5:** Cavan Images; Huntstock/Brand X Pictures; skynesher/E+; SolStock/E+; Morsa Images/E+; Klaus Vedfelt/DigitalVision; Imgorthand/E+; Compassionate Eye Foundation/Robert Kent/DigitalVision; Peter Garrard; Beck/The Image Bank; Monty Rakusen/Image Source; **U6:** South_agency/E+; Yellow Dog Productions/Photodisc; Pgiam/E+; Jaroslav Siroky/EyeEm; Yevgen Romanenko/

Moment; Helen King/The Image Bank; Martin Harvey/The Image Bank; Janmejaysinh Jadeja/EyeEm; Sen Lin Photography/Moment; Reinhard Dirscherl/The Image Bank; Nicolas Reusens/Moment; Paul Mödden/EyeEm; David Malan/Stone; Colin Langford/500px Prime; **U7:** Tony Anderson/Stone; Narisara Nami/Moment; Russ Rohde/Image Source; martin-dm/E+; Darwin Fan/Moment; RgStudio/E+; Barry Winiker/The Image Bank; Paul Burns/DigitalVision; SolStock/E+; Morsa Images/DigitalVision; ljubaphoto/E+; Theo Wargo/Getty Images Entertainment; **U8:** Peter Dazeley/The Image Bank; fotograzia/Moment; Radoslav Zilinsky/Moment; Wattanaphob Kappago/EyeEm; Compassionate Eye Foundation/Steven Errico/DigitalVision; Carles Navarro Parcerisas/Moment; Enis Aksoy/DigitalVision Vectors; cnythzl/DigitalVision Vectors; appleuzr/DigitalVision Vectors; Jupiterimages/The Image Bank; Luis Alvarez/DigitalVision; MoMo Productions/DigitalVision; **Rev:** Thomas Barwick/DigitalVision; Vincent Besnault/The Image Bank; Drazen_/E+; SDI Productions/E+; Allan Baxter/The Image Bank; Westend61; Stocktrek/Photodisc; **GrR:** Klaus Vedfelt/DigitalVision; Eduardo Gonzalez Diaz/EyeEm; Lisa Mei Photography/Moment; Cavan Images; SolStock/E+; **SpB:** Tim Graham/Getty Images News; George Rose/Getty Images News; ullstein bild; Monty Rakusen/Image Source; Daniel Mihailescu/AFP.

The following photographs are sourced from another library:

U2: Guy Bell/Alamy Stock Photo; Yon Marsh/Alamy Stock Photo; **U3:** Louis Berk/Alamy Stock Photo; Madhouse/Happinet/Photo 12/Alamy Stock Photo; Ron Harvey/Everett Collection Inc/Alamy Stock Photo; BFA/Alamy Stock Photo; **U8:** Xinhua/Alamy Stock Photo.

Cover photography by DisobeyArt/iStock/Getty Images Plus.

Illustration
Illustrations by Hyphen.

Animations
Grammar animation Video production by QBS Learnings. Voiceover by Dan Strauss.

Audio
Audio production by Leon Chambers.

Typesetting
Typesetting by Hyphen.

URLs
The publisher has used its best endeavours to ensure that the URLs for external websites referred to in this book are correct and active at the time of going to press. However, the publisher has no responsibility for the websites and can make no guarantee that a site will remain live or that the content is or will remain appropriate.